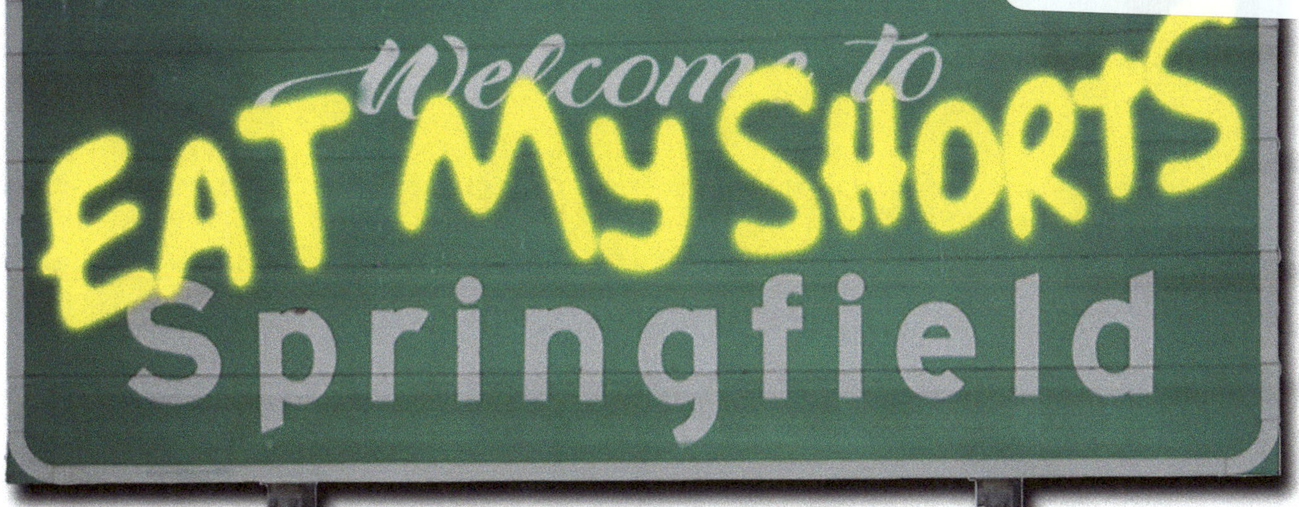

By CHRIS 51

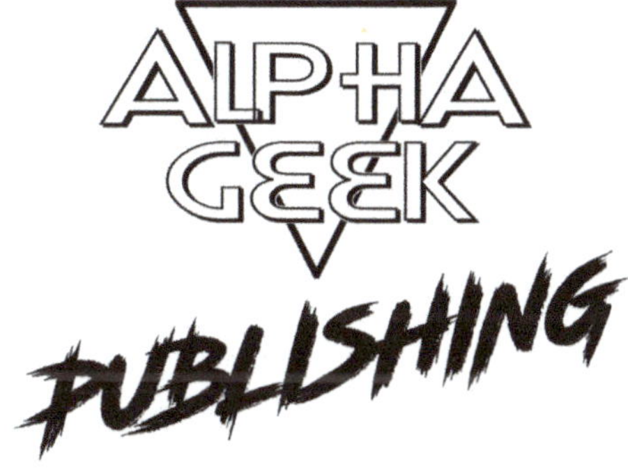

ISBN 978-1-5136-4849-1
ALPHA GEEK PUBLISHING
3585 Main St.
Springfield, OR 97478
CHRIS 51
email-Chris@chris51.com

FOR MATT GROENING
AND FOX NETWORK
THANKS FOR DECADES OF...
ENTERTAINMENT
INSPIRATION
LAUGHTER
LOYALTY
HARD WORK
INGENUITY
MOTIVATION
AND FOR...
STICKING TO YOUR GUNS
GOING WITH YOUR GUT
NOT TAKING NO FOR AN ANSWER
NOT FOLLOWING NORMAL RULES
NOT BEING AFRAID TO TRY NEW THINGS
GOING OUT ON A LIMB
RISKING IT ALL
PROVIDING CANON FOR CLICHE DEDICATIONS
AND FOR...
SHOWING RICH SPOILED PEOPLE WHAT REAL FAMILY LIFE IS LIKE
STAYING TRUE TO YOUR CHARACTERS AND NOT JUMPING ON LATEST FADS
NOT RESORTING TO CRUDE STUPID WRITING FOR EXTRA LAUGHS
NOT CHEAPENING THE INTEGRITY OF YOUR CREATIONS
AND ESPECIALLY FOR..
ALWAYS MAKING FUN OF EVERYBODY, EVERY RACE, AND EVERY SOCIETAL CLASS EQUALLY!

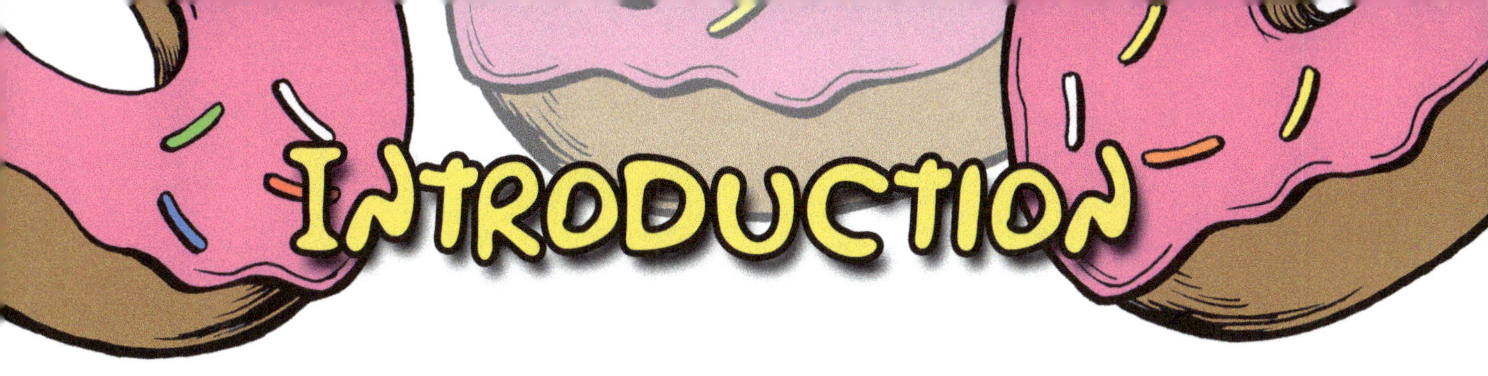

INTRODUCTION

The Simpsons are not just a blue-collar family that we can (and have) all related to. The infamous yellow family is a time traveling, future telling, life-changing American staple. They are more than just a cultural phenomena spanning over three decades. The Simpsons are more *real* and relatable than most human-powered comedy sitcoms, and continue to touch our hearts and tickle our funny bones on a weekly prime time daily basis.

Aside from laughter and nostalgia, The Simpsons inspire a world of creation from the most acclaimed professional artists to armature aficionados. Whether its seen in museums on canvas, pages of a comic, or in the flesh with tattoos: Simpsons art is a yellow force to be reckoned with.

Artist Chris 51 has been addicted to the *allure of the yellow* since day one. “The Simpsons are half the reason I became an artist in the first place,” he explains. Chris is world-renown for tattooing the most flawless recreations of Simpson characters; having performed his craft on rock stars, celebrities and thousands of fans. Chris himself has Simpsons characters tattooed on his hands, legs, arms, Milhouse riding a bald eagle across his chest, (the most famous) pink donut tattoo around his belly button (as seen on A&E’s Epic Ink) and even Blinkie on his ball-sack. Now that’s dedication...or stupidity!

“The Simpsons have taken me around the world with my art, and I am so grateful to Matt Groening and everyone involved for giving my generation, and future generations such a positive gift of entertainment and inspiration,” Chris says. “They have also allowed me to rock out, geek out and party with many of my idols in entertainment.”

Chris gets commission requests from fans, peers and families daily to “Simpsonize” them. His original art portfolio has now grown to include comics, books, paintings and gallery exhibits.

“I hope you enjoy viewing the art in this book as much as I enjoyed creating it,” says Chris, “Stay Yellow!”

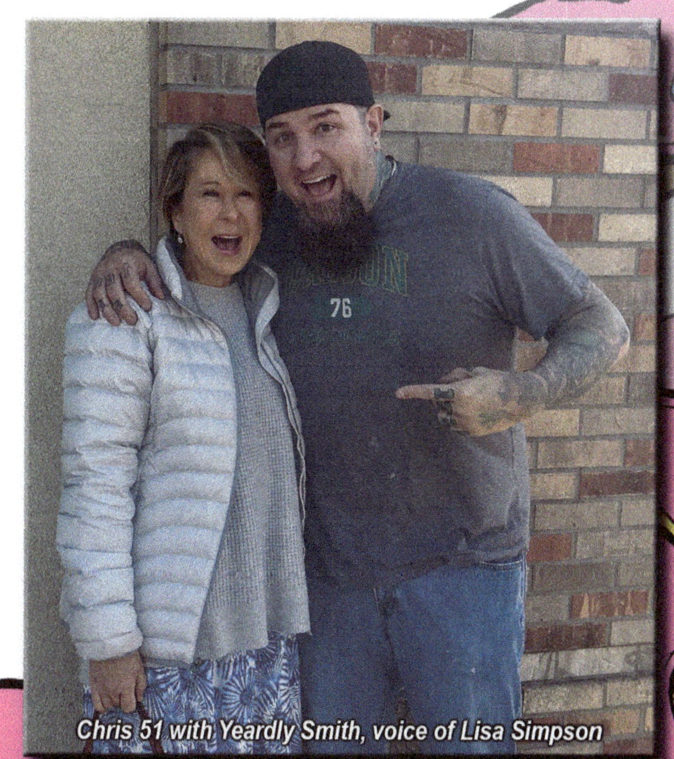

Chris 51 with Yeardly Smith, voice of Lisa Simpson

Chapter 1

Paintings

Although I don't get a chance to create them to often because of time restraints, painting my Simpson portrait renditions is my absolute most favorite thing to do! If I had my little way, I would paint The Simpsons every day, and twice on Sundays, while eating peaches in the shade.

I went in to each painting with the intention of keeping them very loose, almost abstract. But, my style and passion for each character's true likeness kept reverting them back to more life-like versions of their original nature. So, they all ended up like exaggerated realistic cartoon versions of themselves.

Most of these paintings are oil on canvas with acrylic backgrounds. I used damp sponges to get a vintage stylized backdrop and keep it muddled, so all the detail would remain focused on each character.

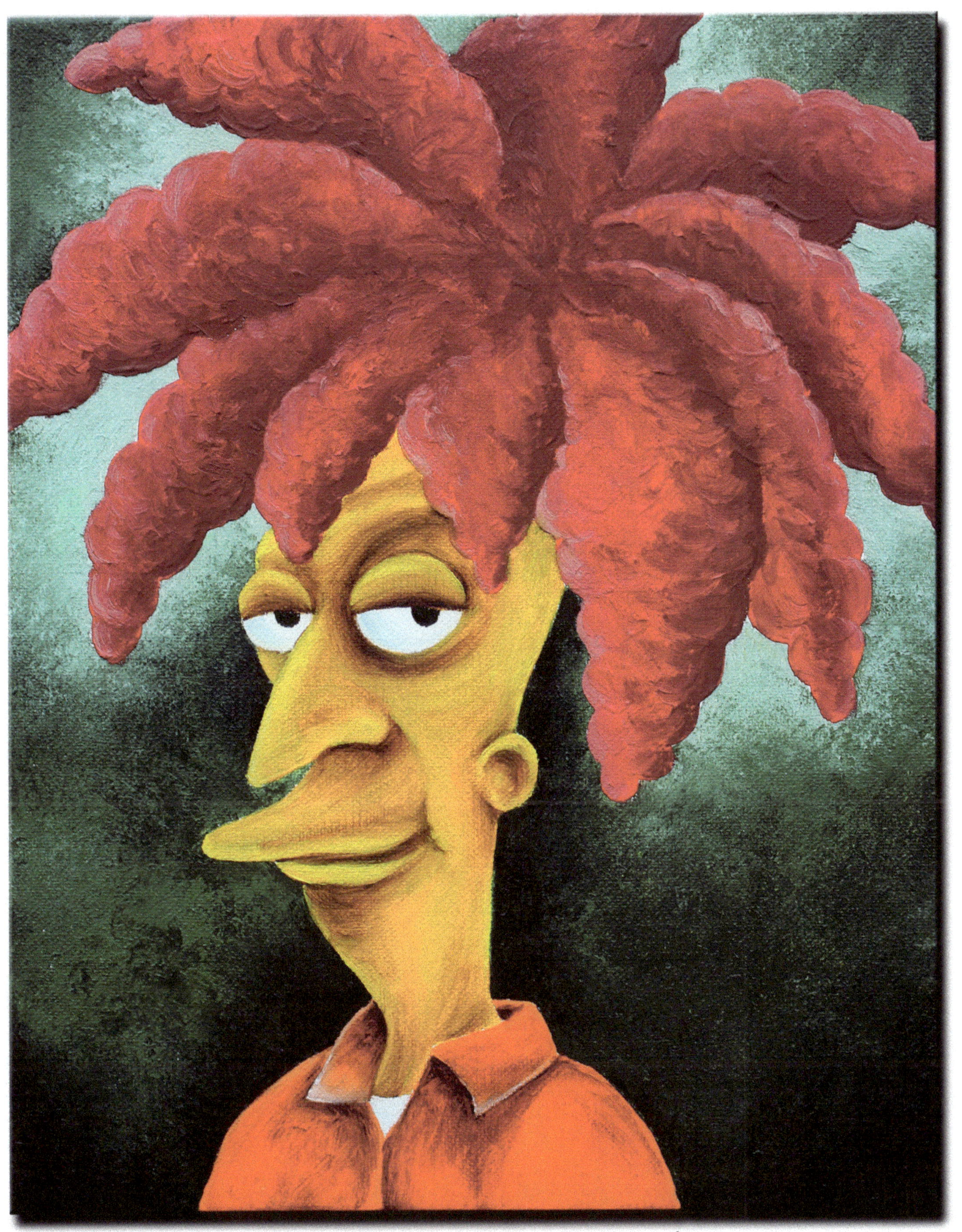

ARROGANT MANIACAL MASTERMIND
Oil & Acrylic on canvas

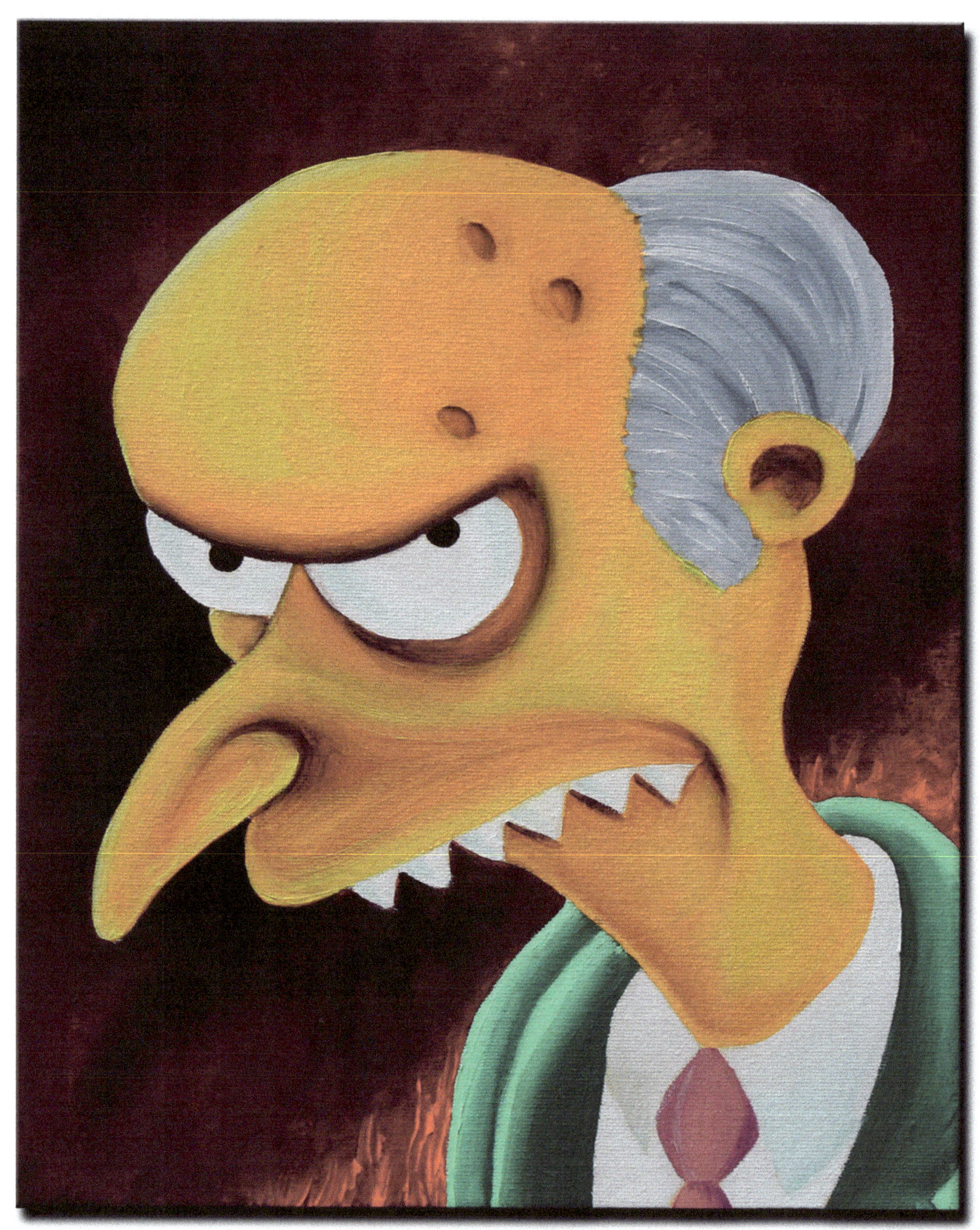

EVIL BUSINESS TYCOON
Oil & Acrylic on canvas

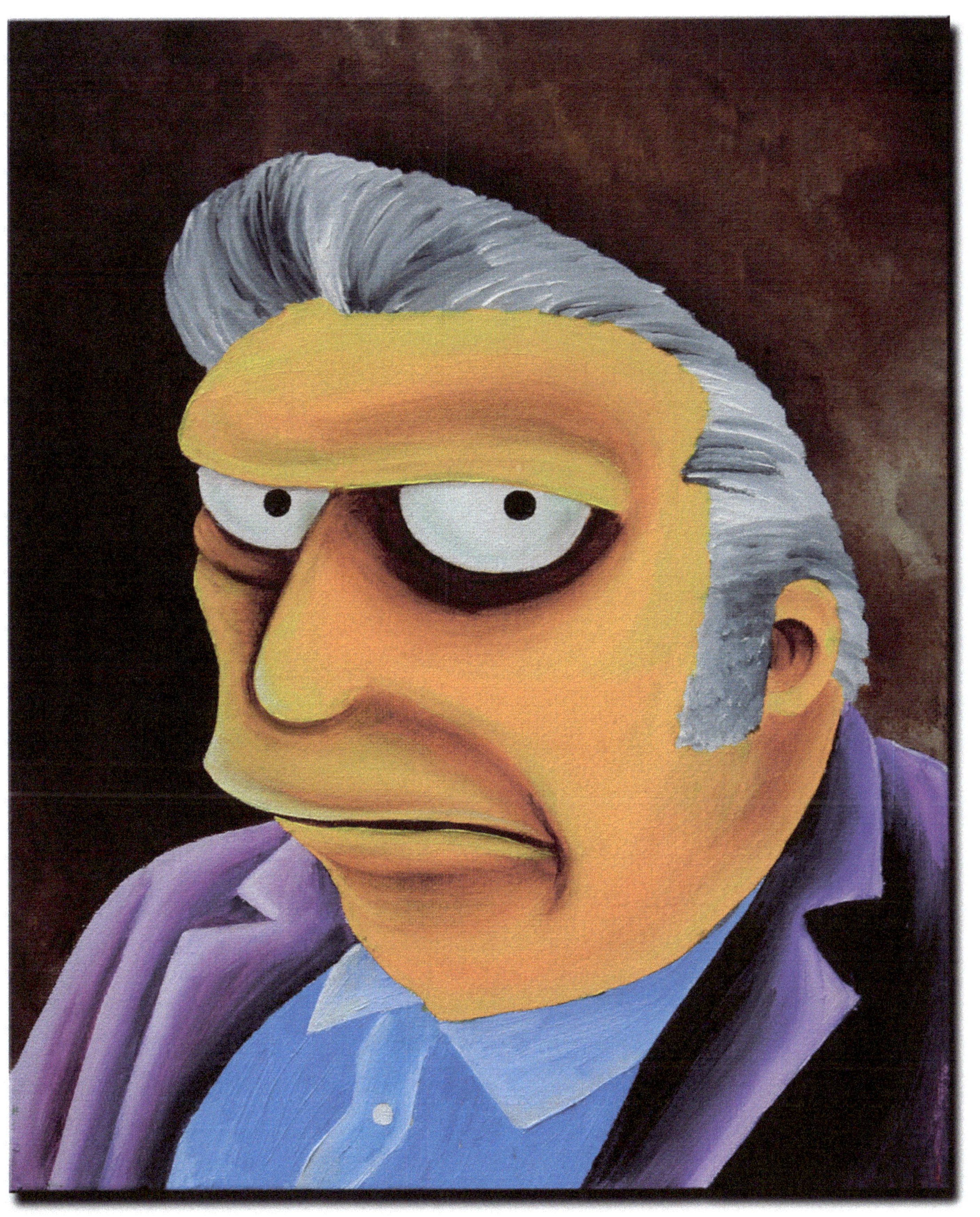

Overweight Mob Boss
Oil & Acrylic on canvas

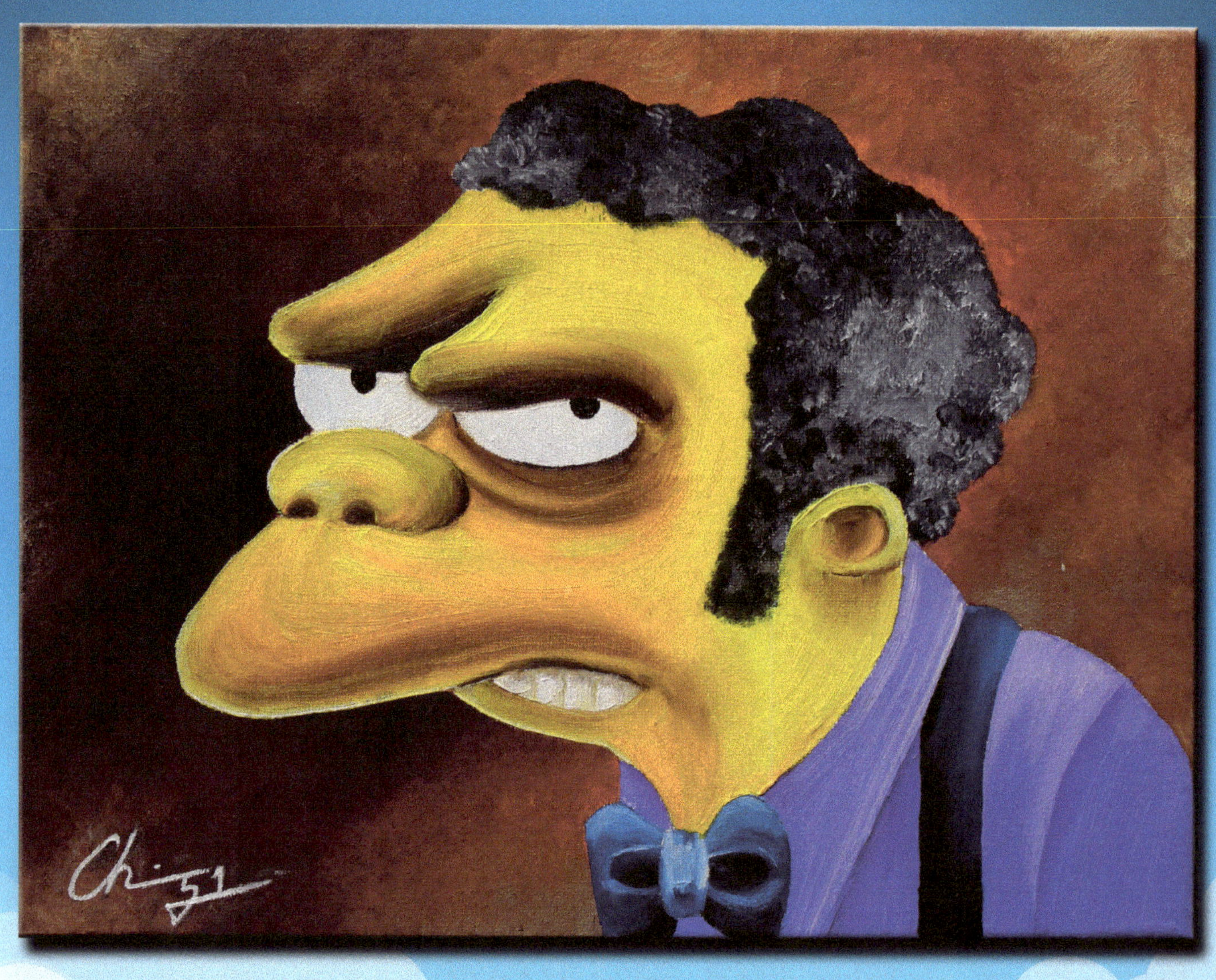

Disgruntled Bartender
Oil & Acrylic on canvas

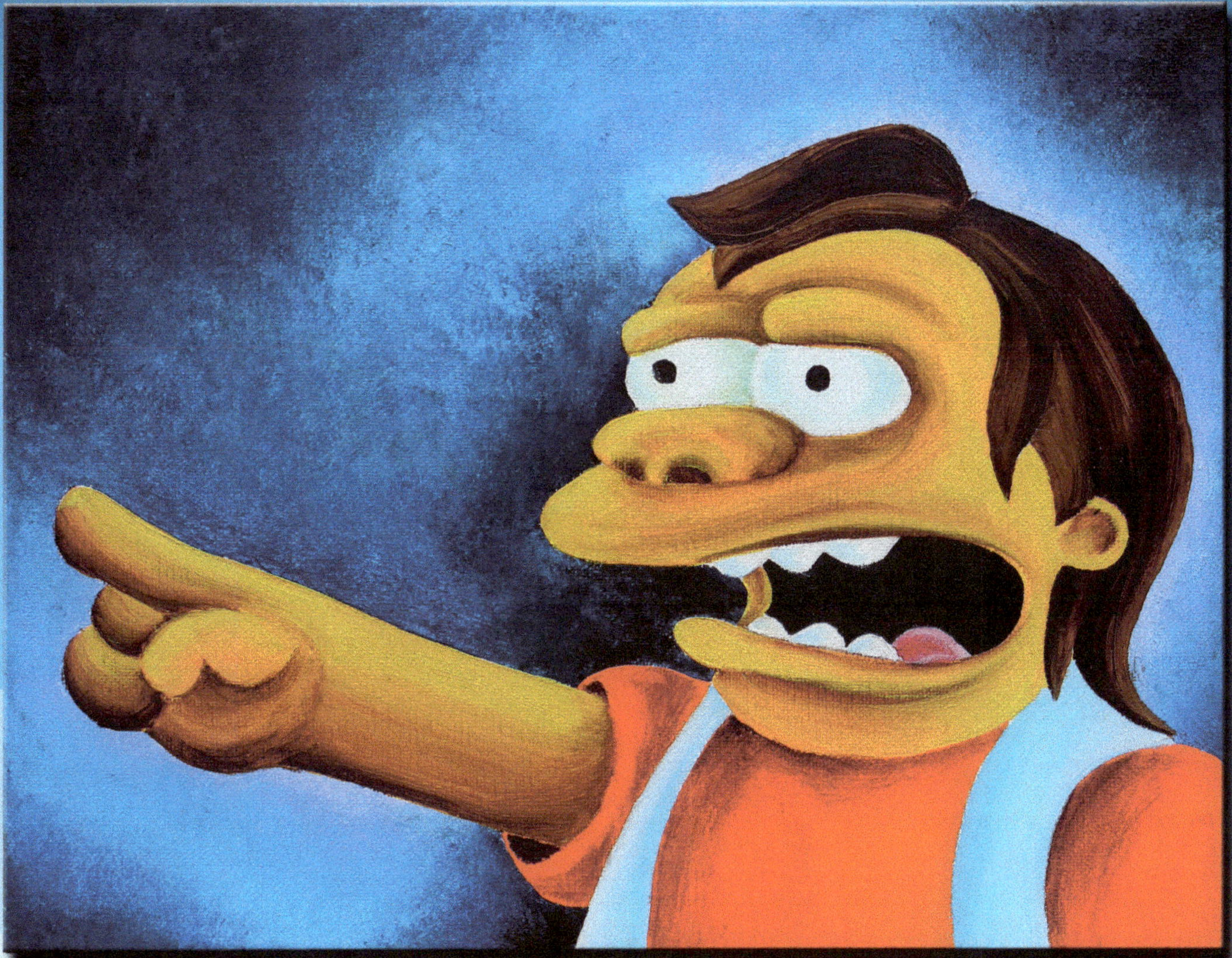

PUDGY INSECURE BULLY
Oil & Acrylic on canvas

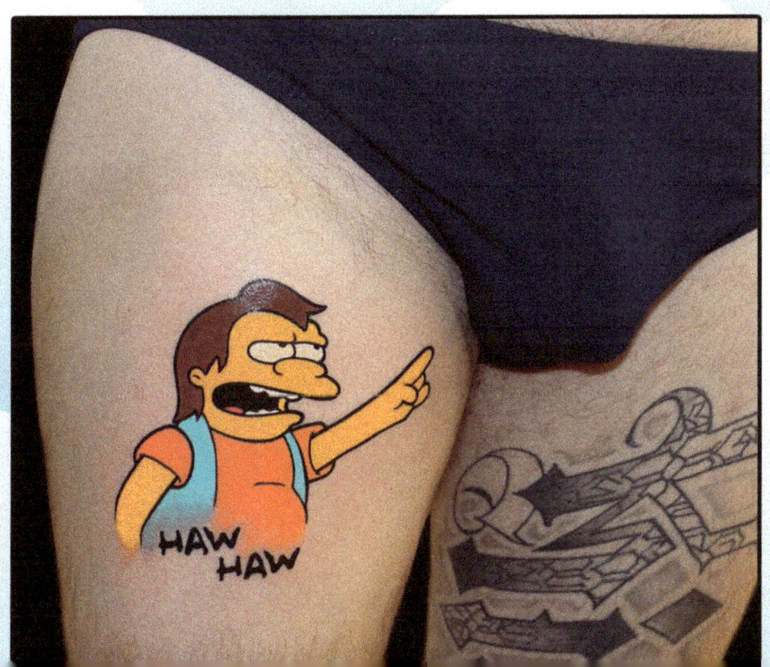

I've had the pleasure of recreating Nelson twice; once on canvas and once in skin. The canvas was an attempt to make Nelson more life-like and three dimensional but still keep the integrity of the original classic look and pose. The tattoo was on a hilarious client, and actually got kicked off of Instagram, being reported for indecency, so I proceeded to post a collage of half-naked women (that they routinely accept) along with my photo of Nelson but blurring out my client's package.

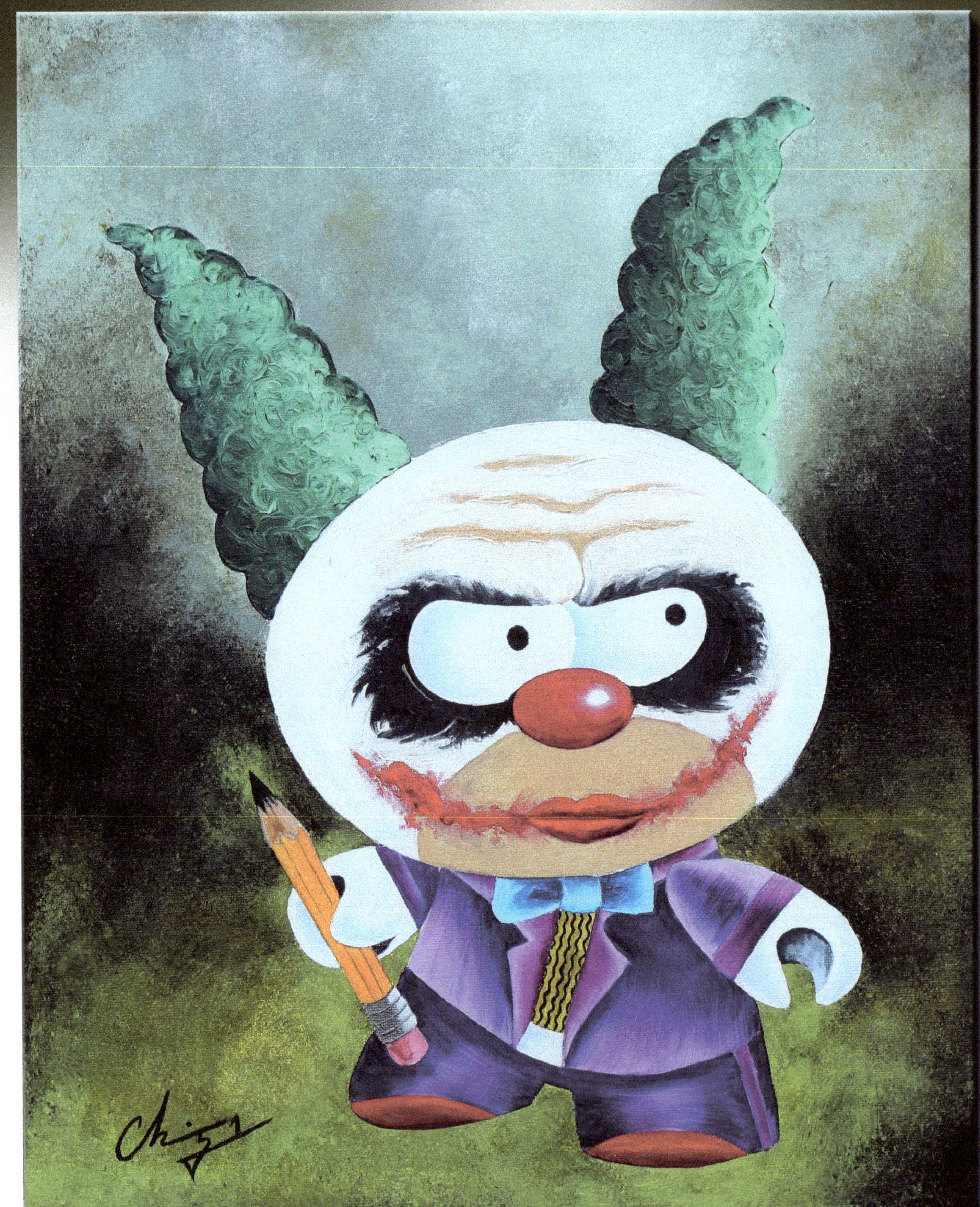

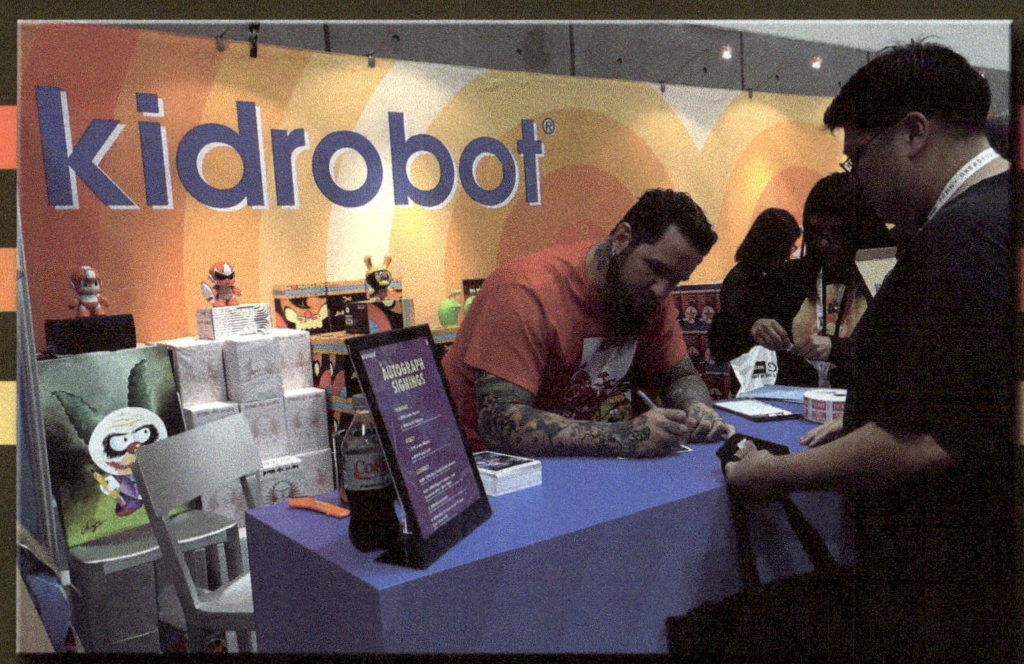

Why So Krusty (adjacent page) was a three-way mash-up of Batman's Joker, Simpson's Krusty the Clown, and Kidrobot's own Dunny toy. While I was sponsored by Kidrobot they asked if I could create a limited edition screen print for San Diego Comic Con in 2015. Since I didn't know crap about screen prints and their layouts/adaptation to art design, I was lost, but I couldn't say no. I asked if I could do an original painting instead, and we could promote it as a giveaway to get fans to stop by the booth and enter to win. They jumped on the idea and the painting went viral that day.

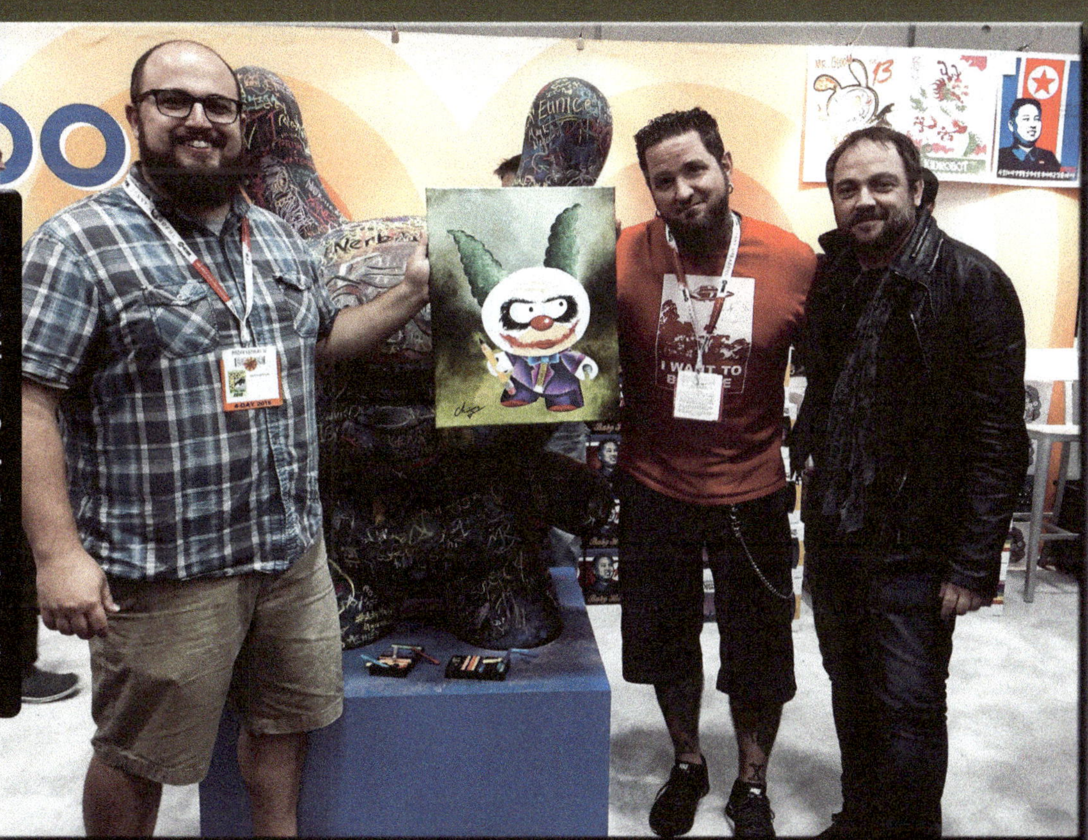

Mark Sheppard (Crowley) from Supernatural is a big KidRobot fan, and loved my *Why So Krusty* painting, so he posed with myself and the winner at San Diego Comic Con.

CHAPTER 2

MUSIC MEMORIALS

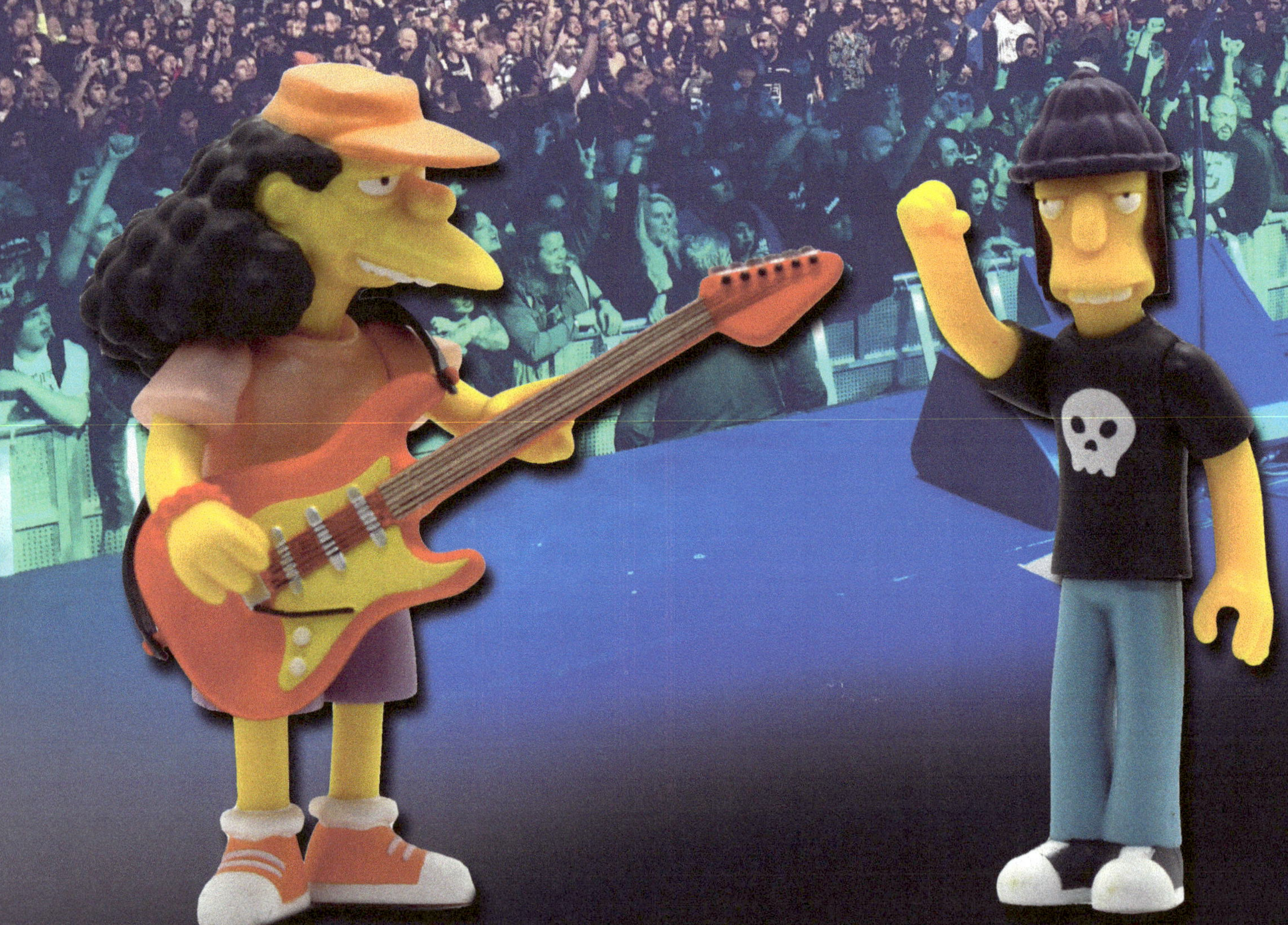

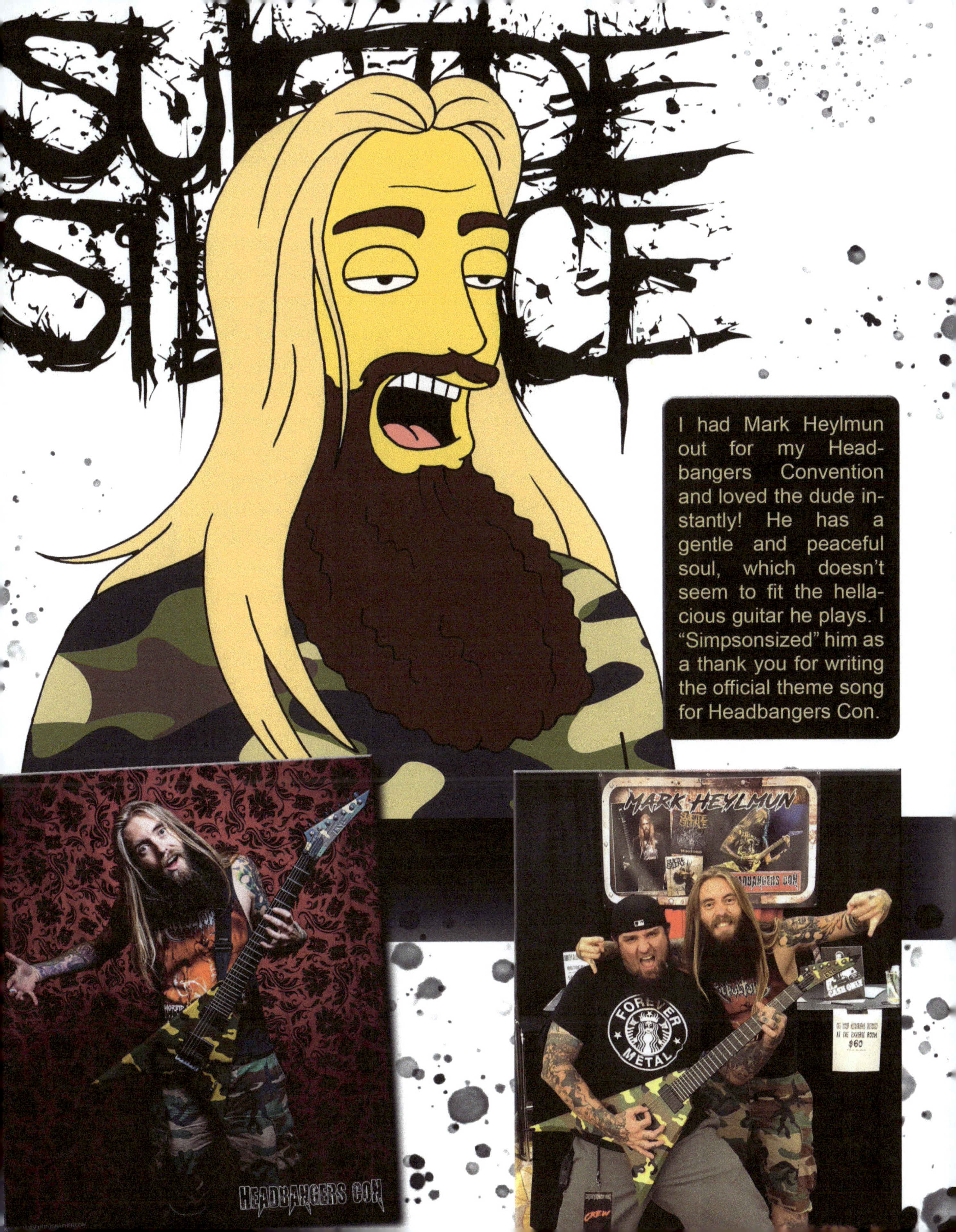

I had Mark Heylmun out for my Headbangers Convention and loved the dude instantly! He has a gentle and peaceful soul, which doesn't seem to fit the hellacious guitar he plays. I "Simpsonsized" him as a thank you for writing the official theme song for Headbangers Con.

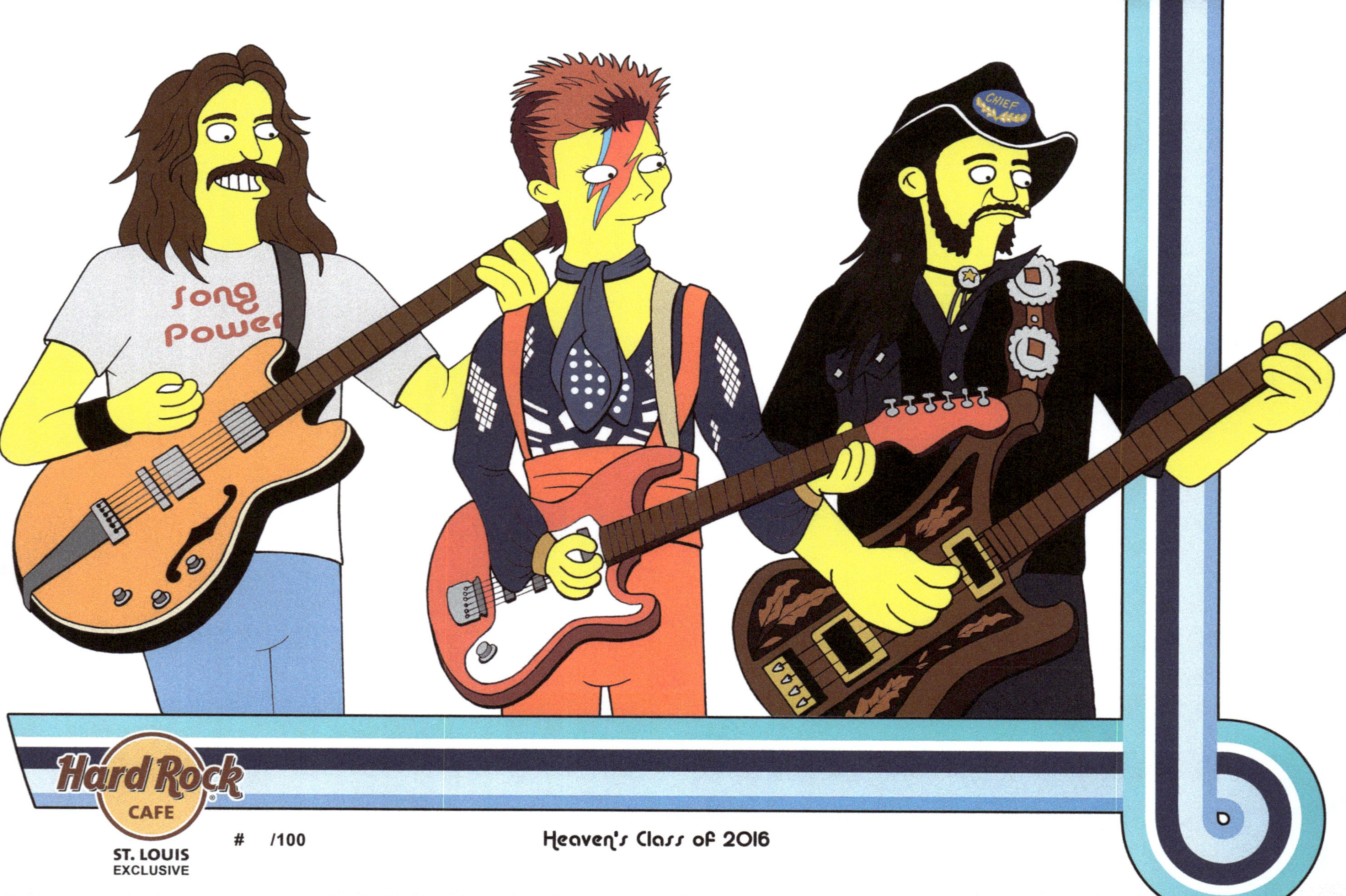
Song
Power
CHIEF
Hard Rock
CAFE
ST. LOUIS
EXCLUSIVE
/100
Heaven's Class of 2016

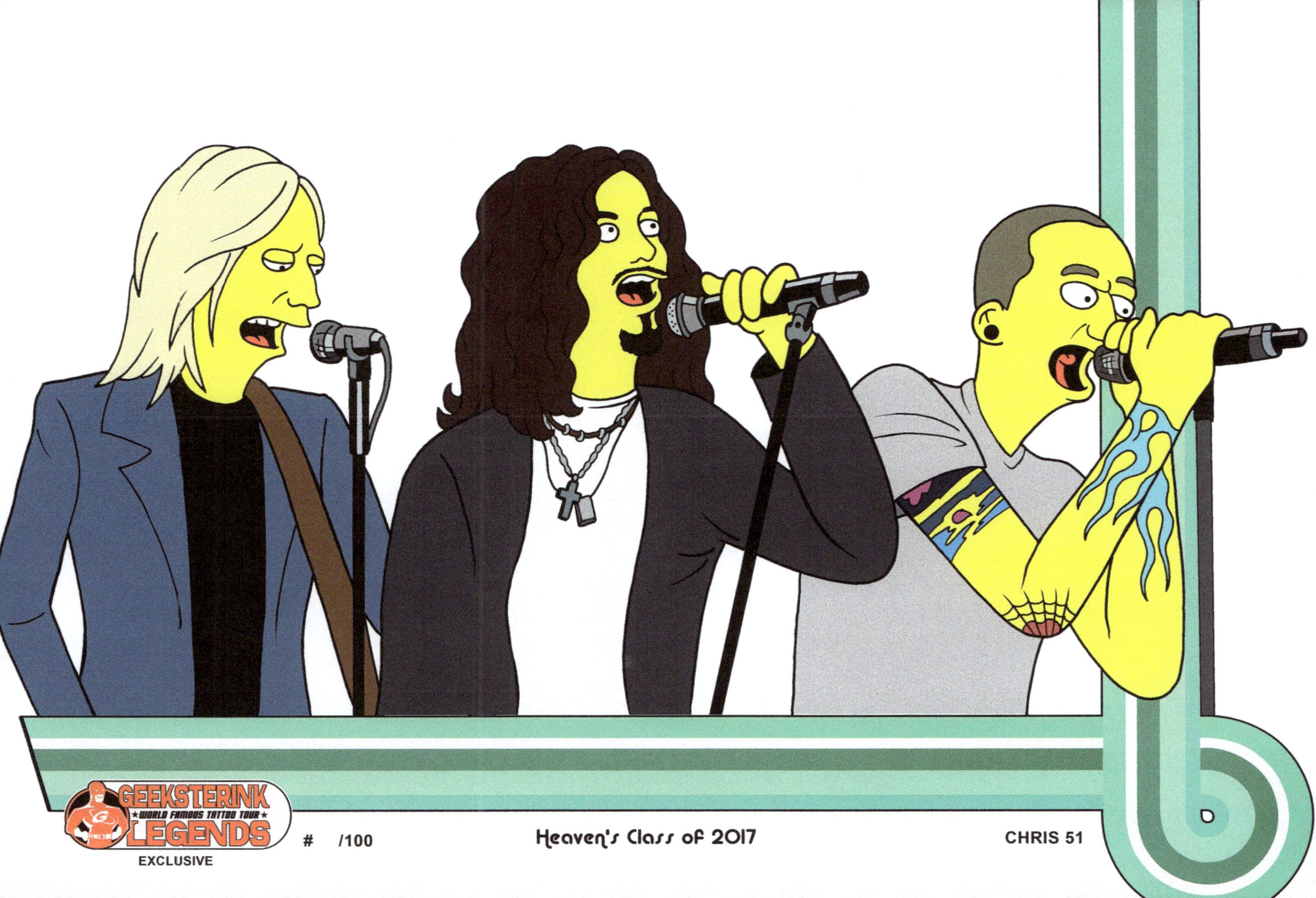
GEEKSTERINK
★WORLD FAMOUS TATTOO TOUR★
LEGENDS
EXCLUSIVE
/100
Heaven's Class of 2017
CHRIS 51

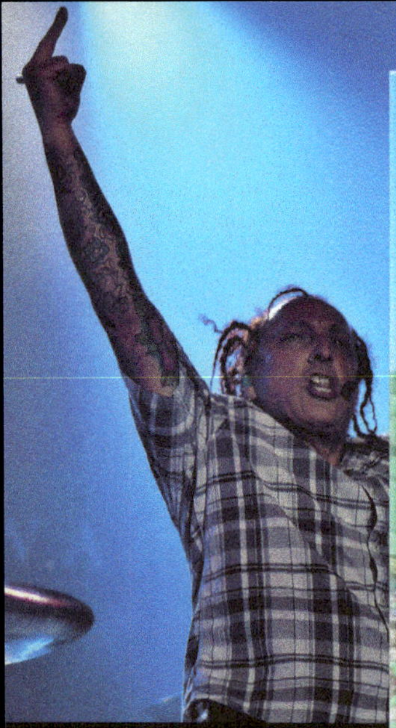

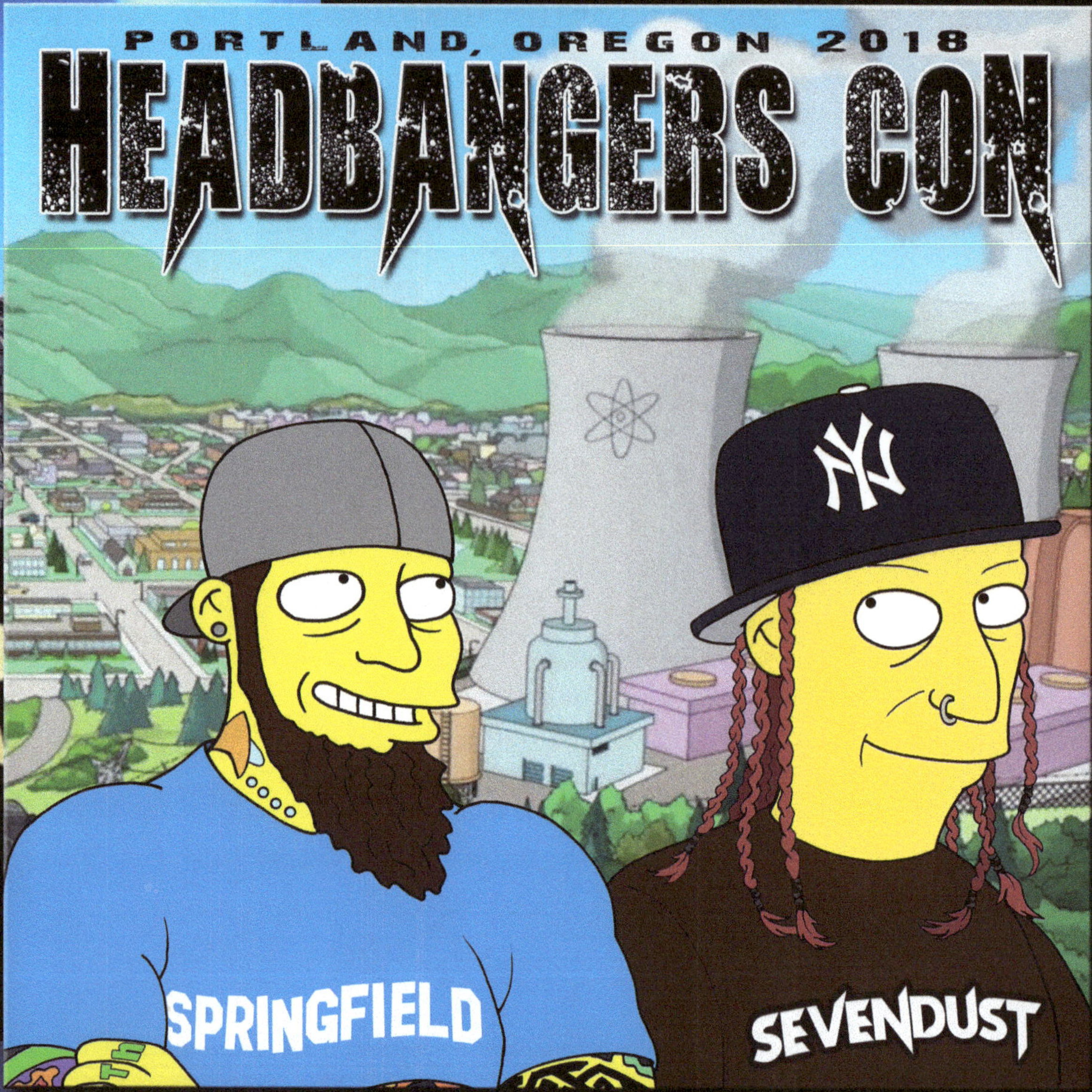

PORTLAND, OREGON 2018

HEADBANGERS CON

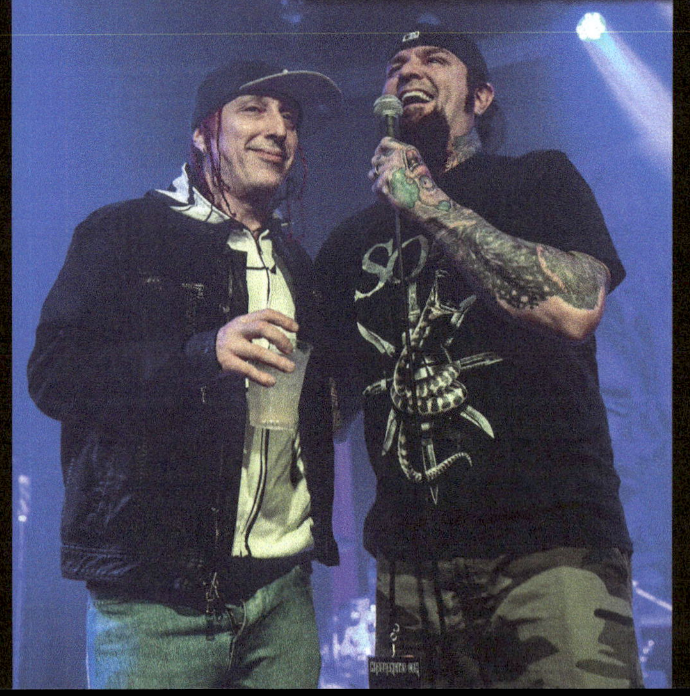

Morgan Rose isn't just one of the best drummers in the world, he's one of my best friends in the world! I met him through our mutual friend Brett who arranged to tattoo him on my new show I was filming, knowing I was a HUGE fan of Sevendust. He signed my foot and Brett tattooed it on the episode. We hit it off immediately, like long lost brothers reacquainted. I invited Morgan to become part owner of a new type of convention I was planning; Headbangers Con. It was a comic con style event but for Metal culture, and it had never been done before. Together we made history doing it, and have several more planned. Morgan is the kindest guy you'll ever meet, and I love him!

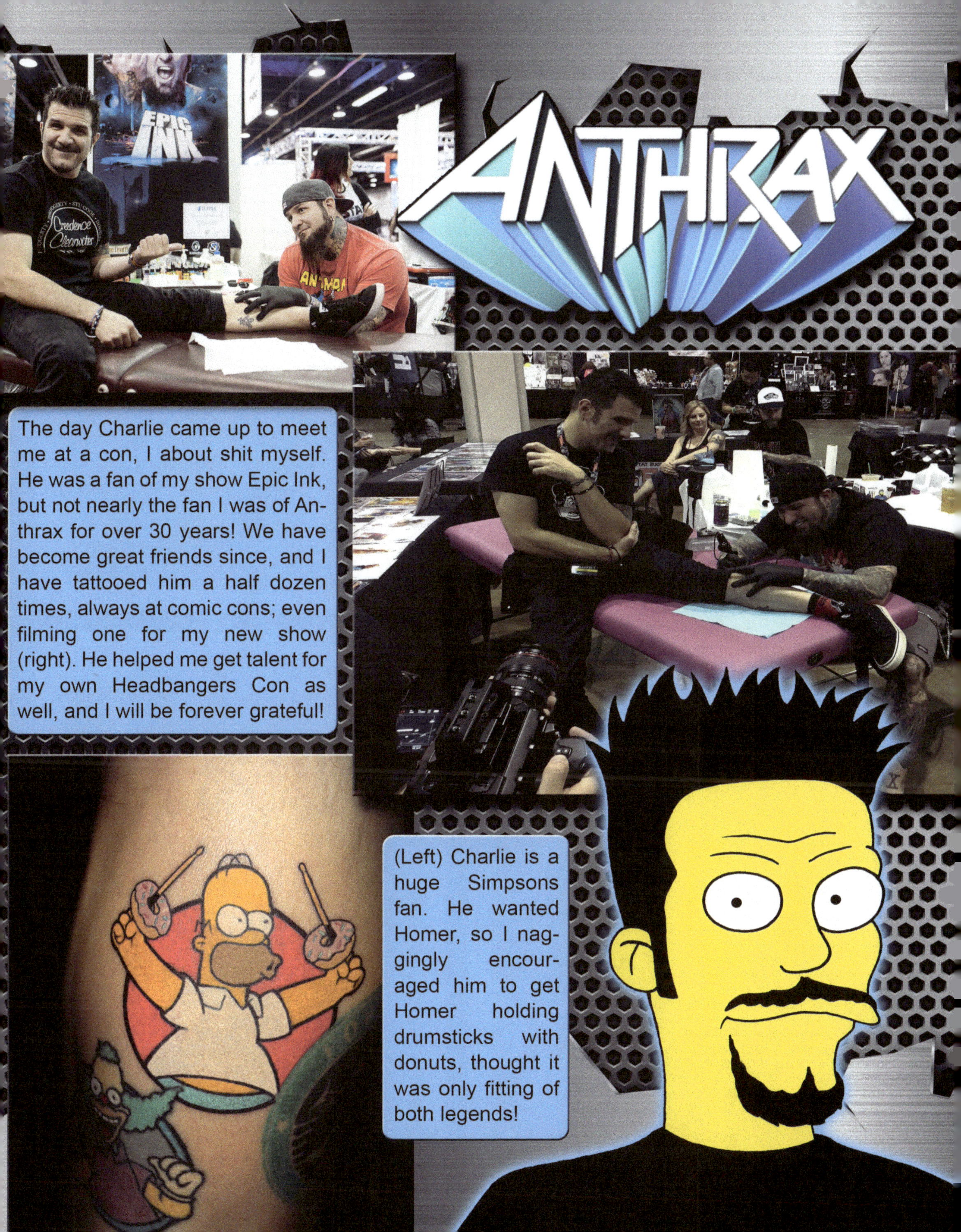

The day Charlie came up to meet me at a con, I about shit myself. He was a fan of my show Epic Ink, but not nearly the fan I was of Anthrax for over 30 years! We have become great friends since, and I have tattooed him a half dozen times, always at comic cons; even filming one for my new show (right). He helped me get talent for my own Headbangers Con as well, and I will be forever grateful!

(Left) Charlie is a huge Simpsons fan. He wanted Homer, so I naggingly encouraged him to get Homer holding drumsticks with donuts, thought it was only fitting of both legends!

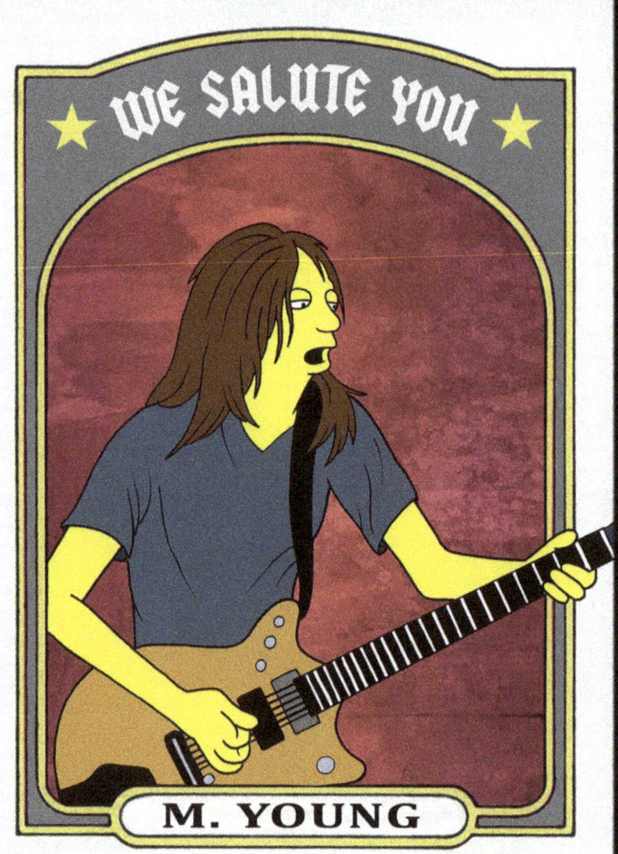
WE SALUTE YOU
M. YOUNG

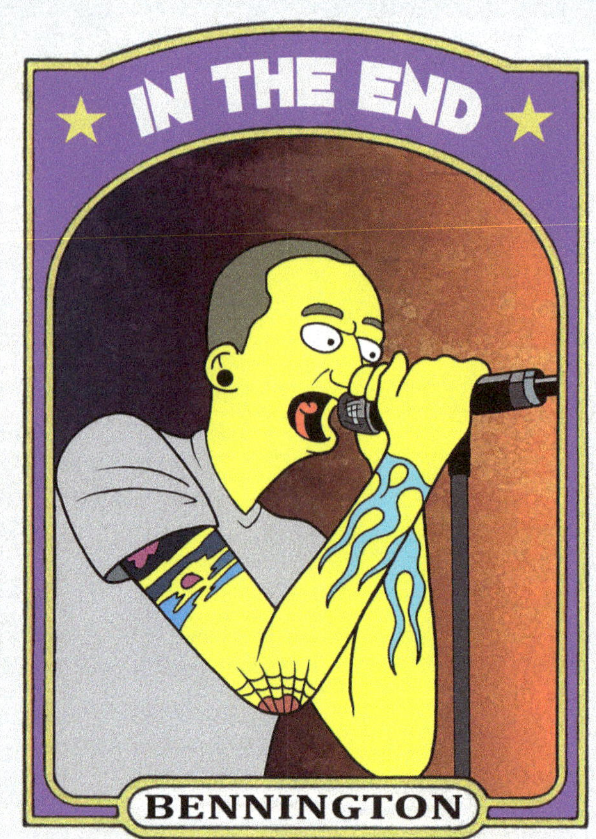
IN THE END
BENNINGTON

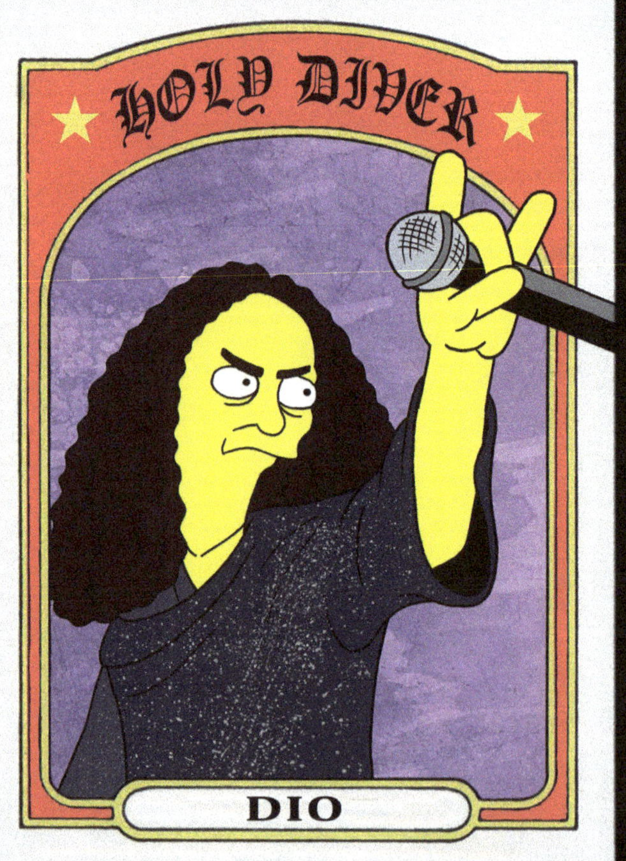
HOLY DIVER
DIO

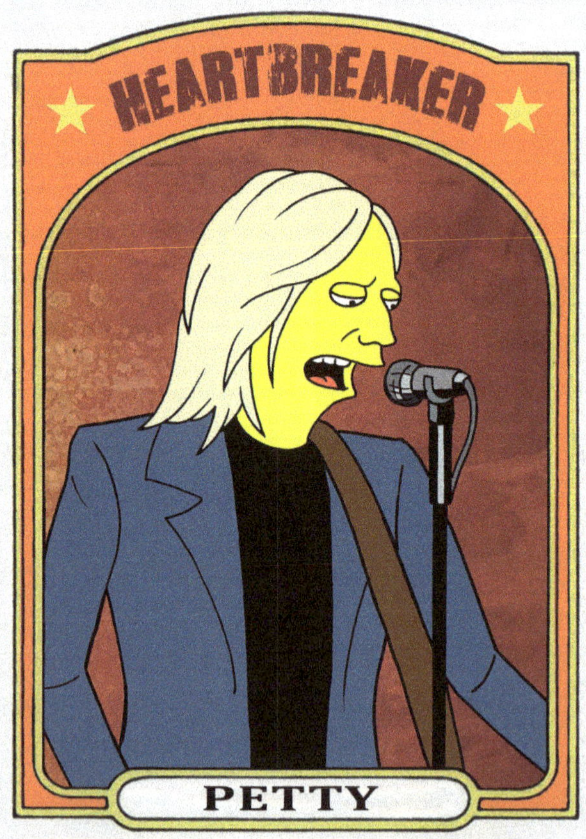
HEARTBREAKER
PETTY

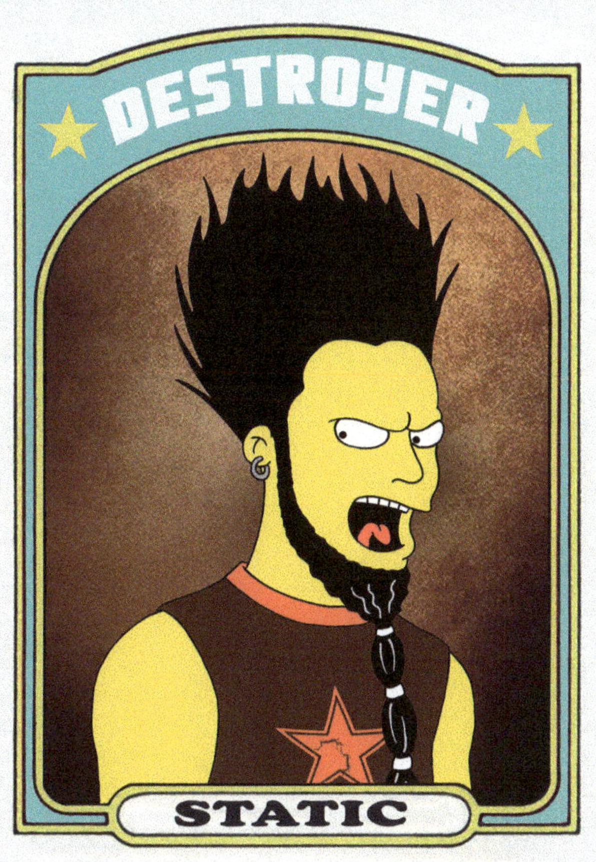
DESTROYER
STATIC

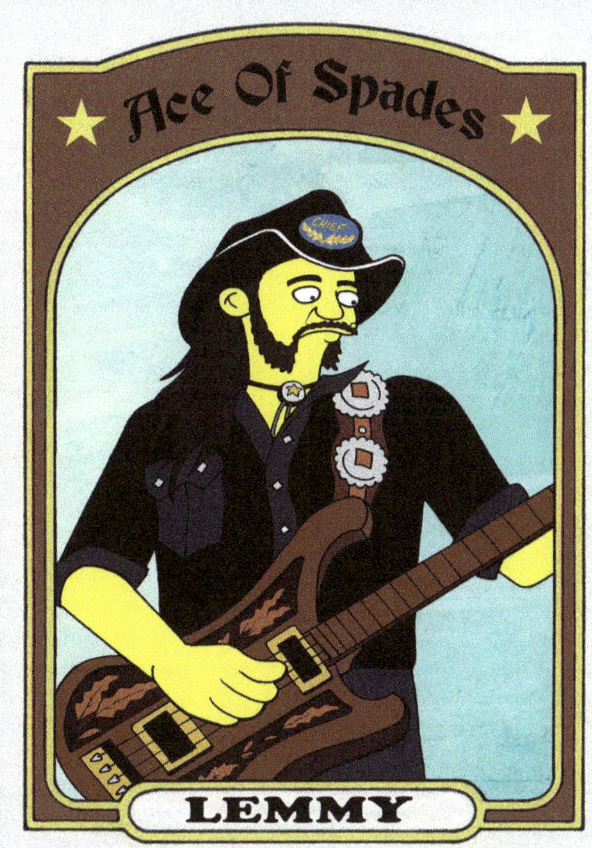
Ace Of Spades
LEMMY

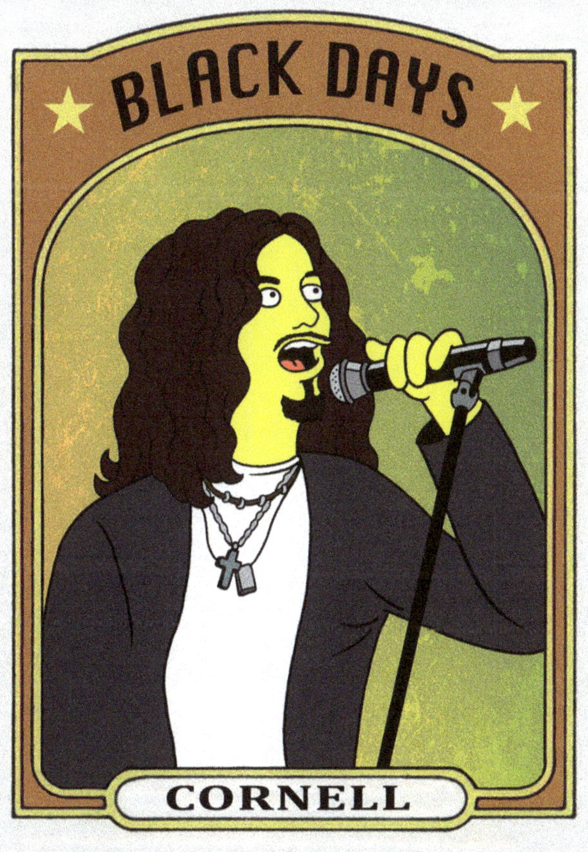
BLACK DAYS
CORNELL

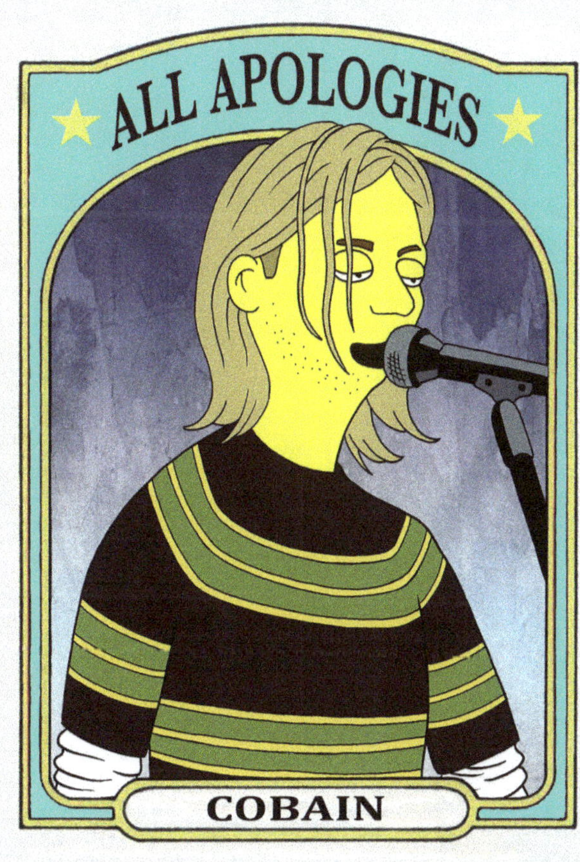
ALL APOLOGIES
COBAIN

Chapter 3

Springfield Strikes Back

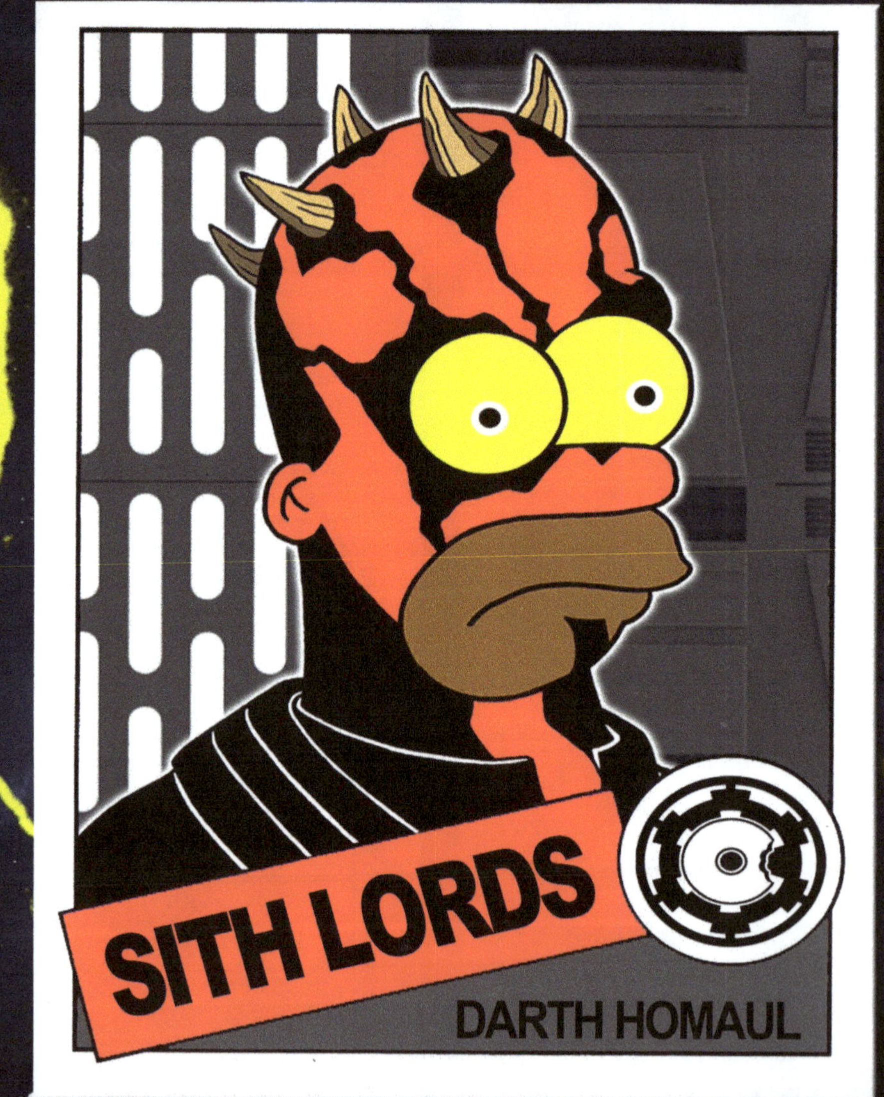

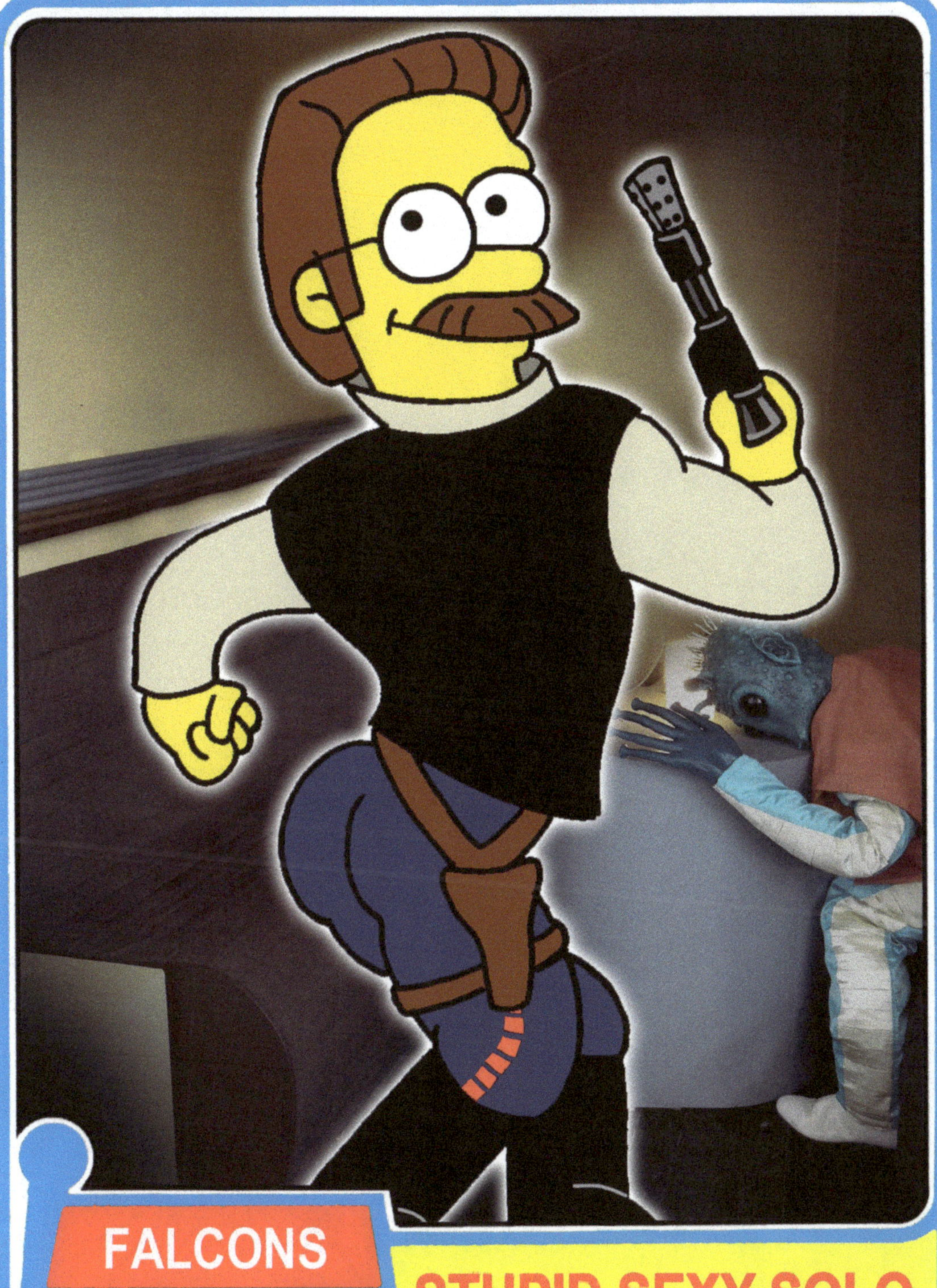
FALCONS
CPT
STUPID SEXY SOLO

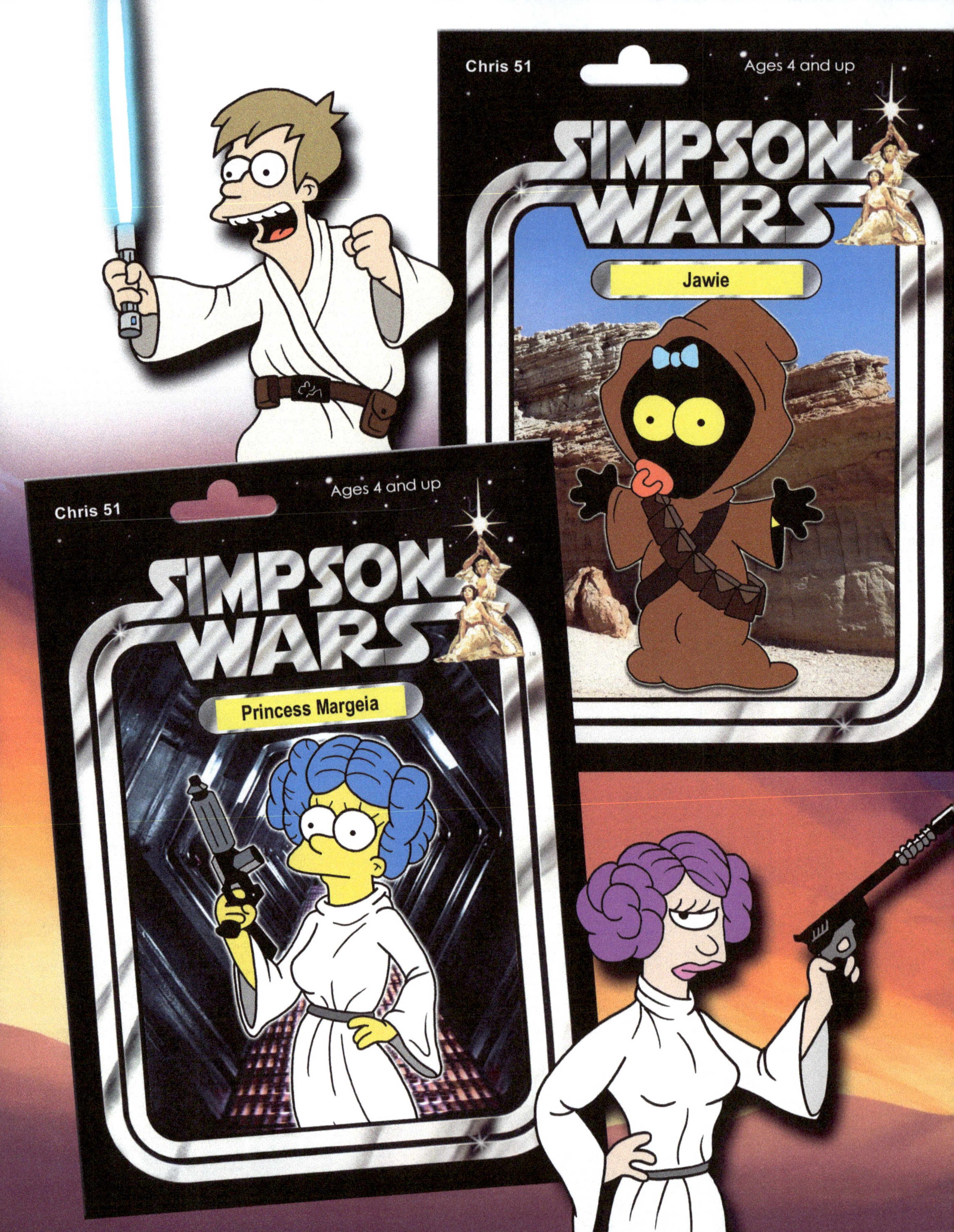
Chris 51
Ages 4 and up
SIMPSON WARS
Jawie
Chris 51
Ages 4 and up
SIMPSON WARS
Princess Margeia

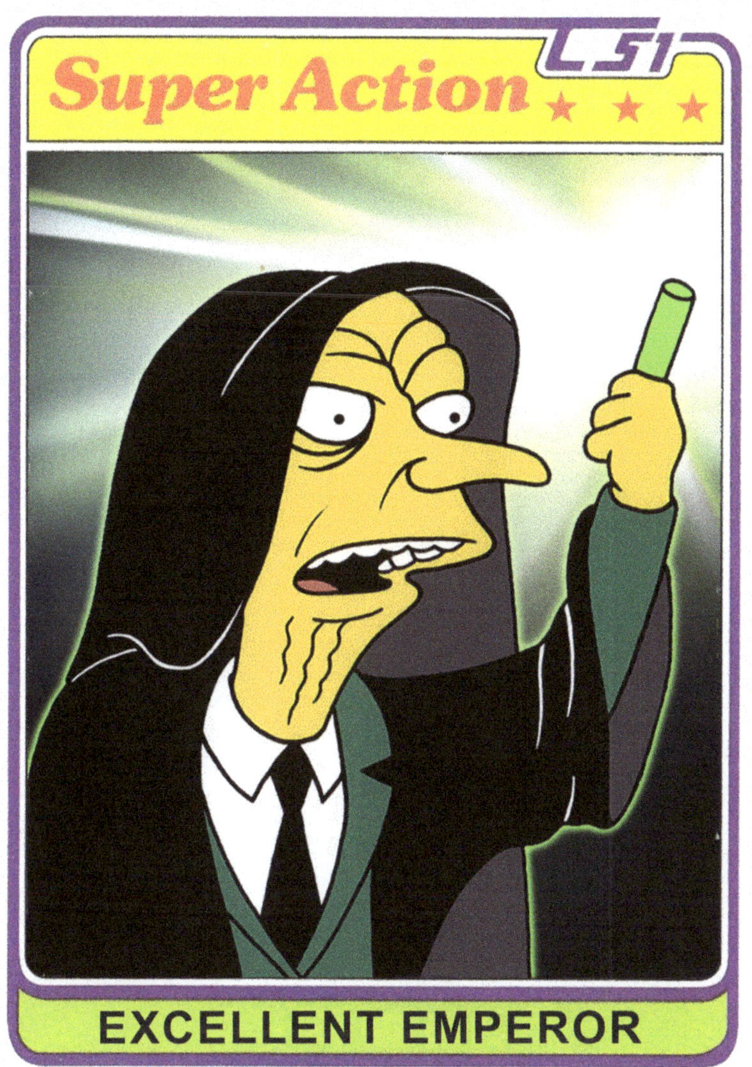
Super Action
CS1
EXCELLENT EMPEROR

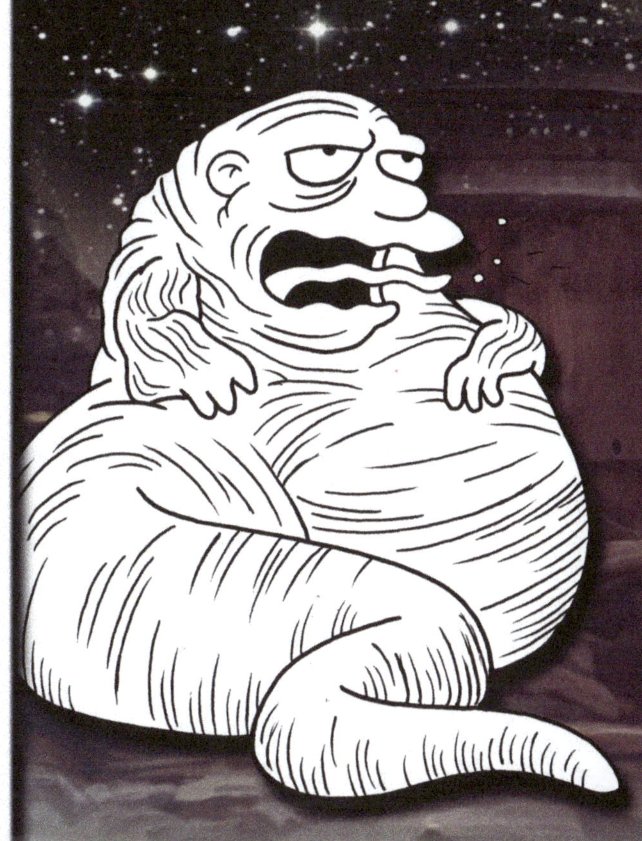

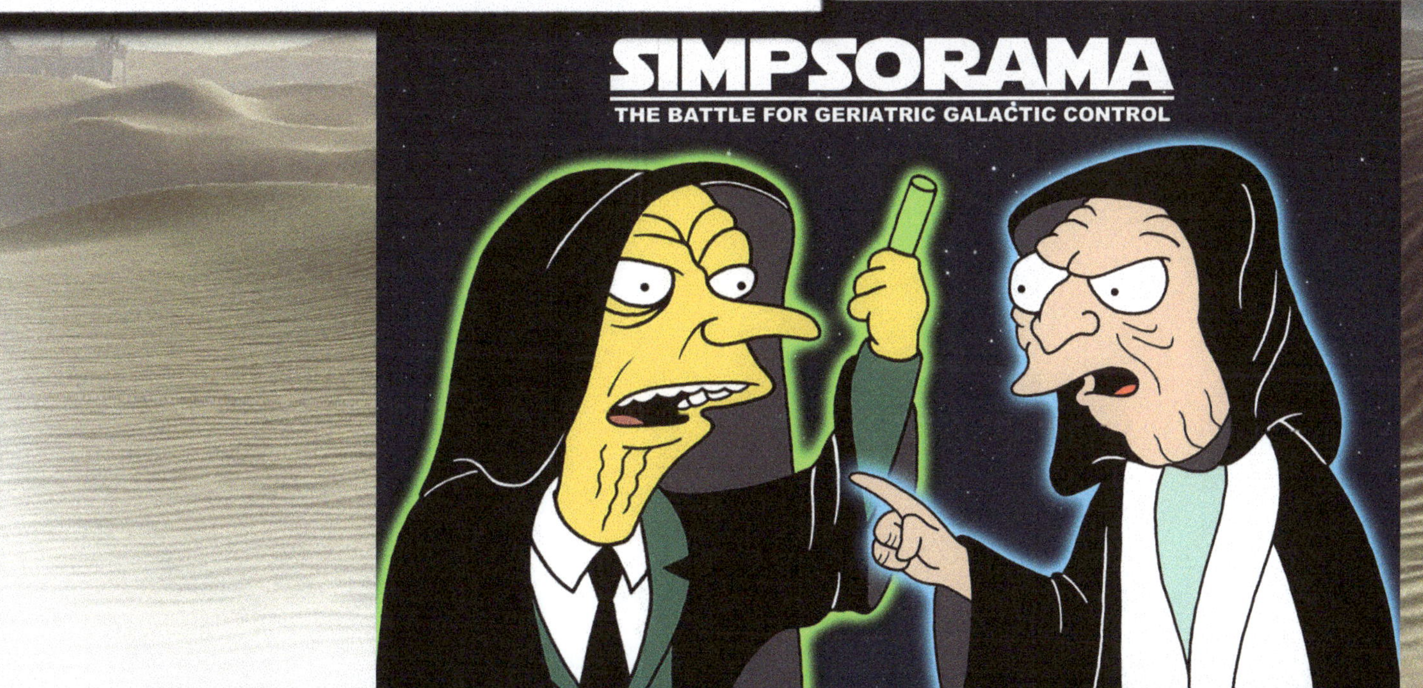
SIMPSORAMA
THE BATTLE FOR GERIATRIC GALACTIC CONTROL

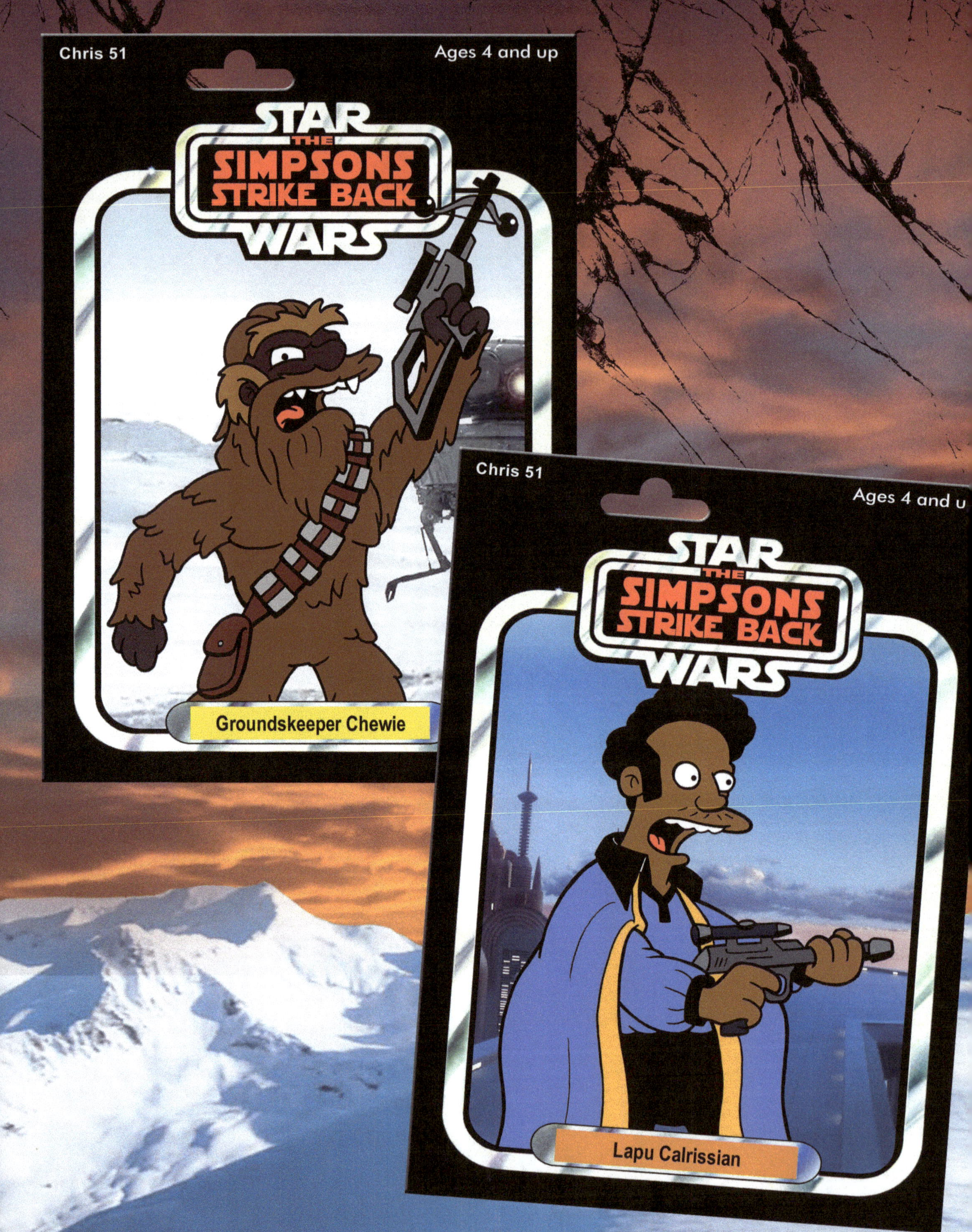
Chris 51
Ages 4 and up
STAR
THE
SIMPSONS
STRIKE BACK
WARS
Groundskeeper Chewie
Chris 51
Ages 4 and u
STAR
THE
SIMPSONS
STRIKE BACK
WARS
Lapu Calrissian

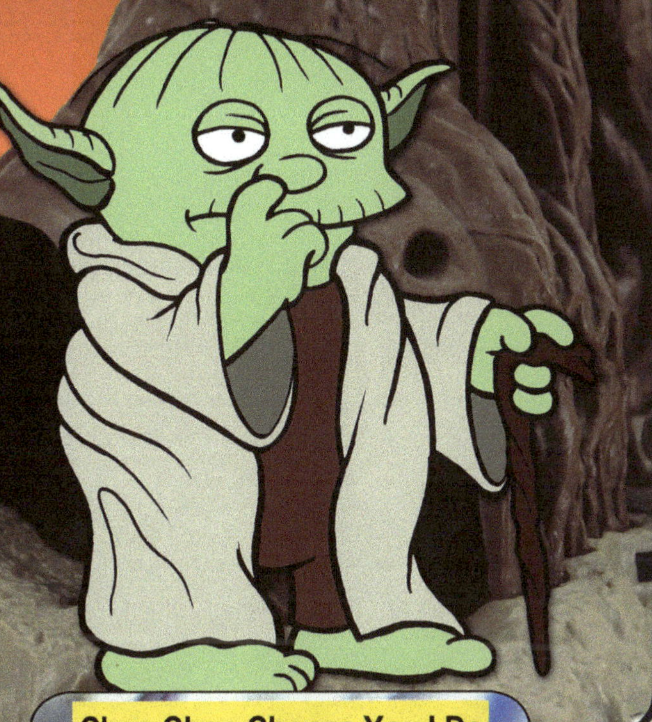
Chris 51
Ages 4 and up
STAR
THE
SIMPSONS
STRIKE BACK
WARS
Choo Choo Choose You I Do

Chris 51

Ages 4 and up

STAR THE SIMPSONS STRIKE BACK WARS

Dark

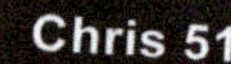

Duff Vader

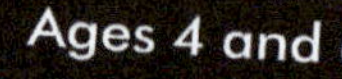

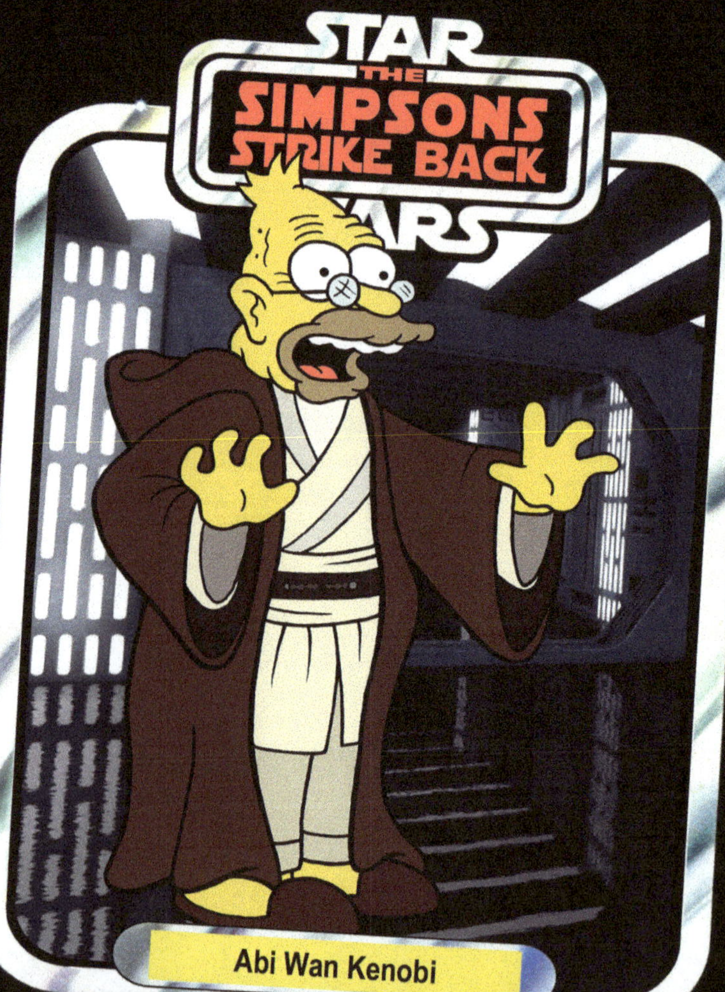

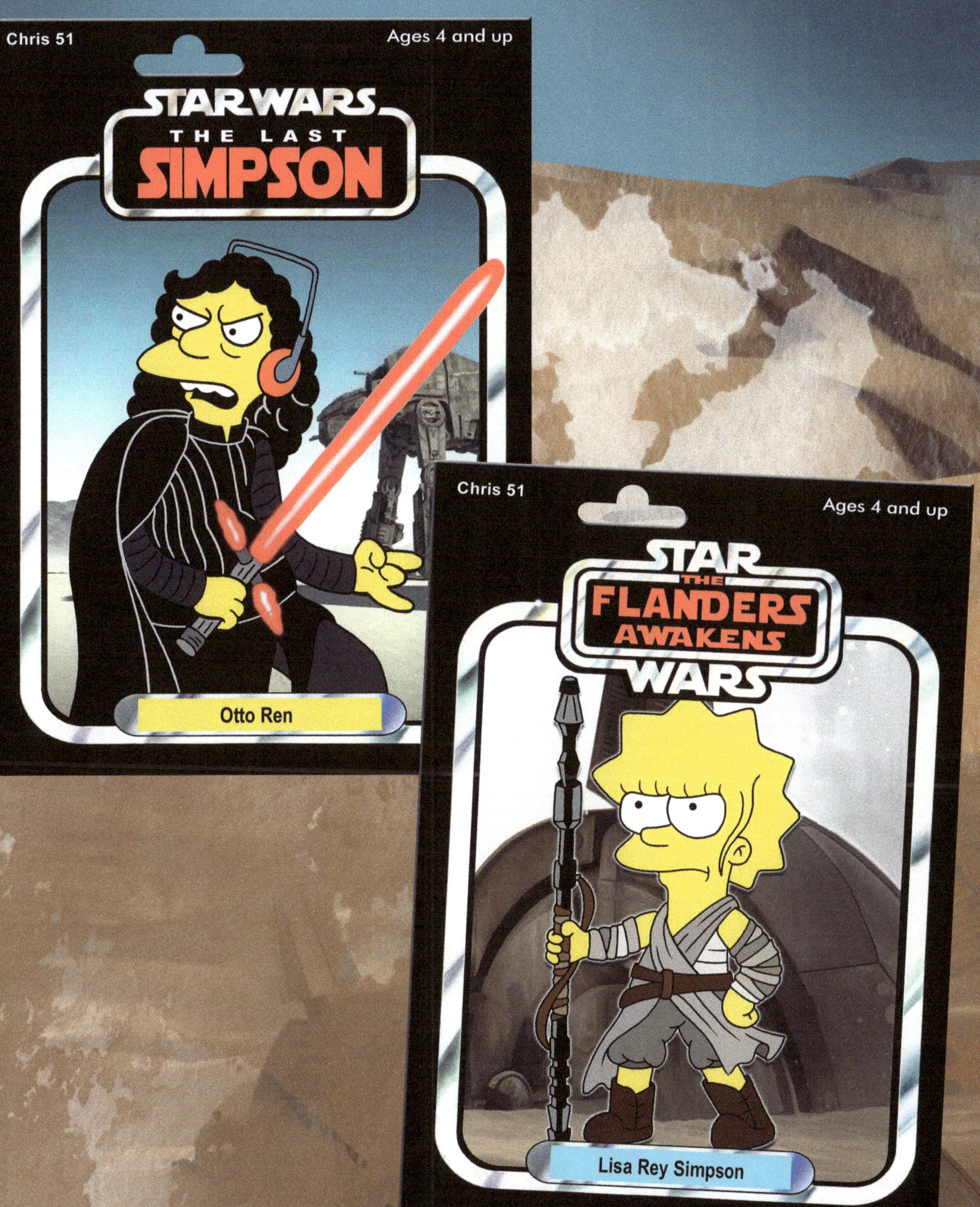
Chris 51
Ages 4 and up
STAR WARS
THE LAST
SIMPSON
Otto Ren
Chris 51
Ages 4 and up
STAR
THE
FLANDERS
AWAKENS
WARS
Lisa Rey Simpson

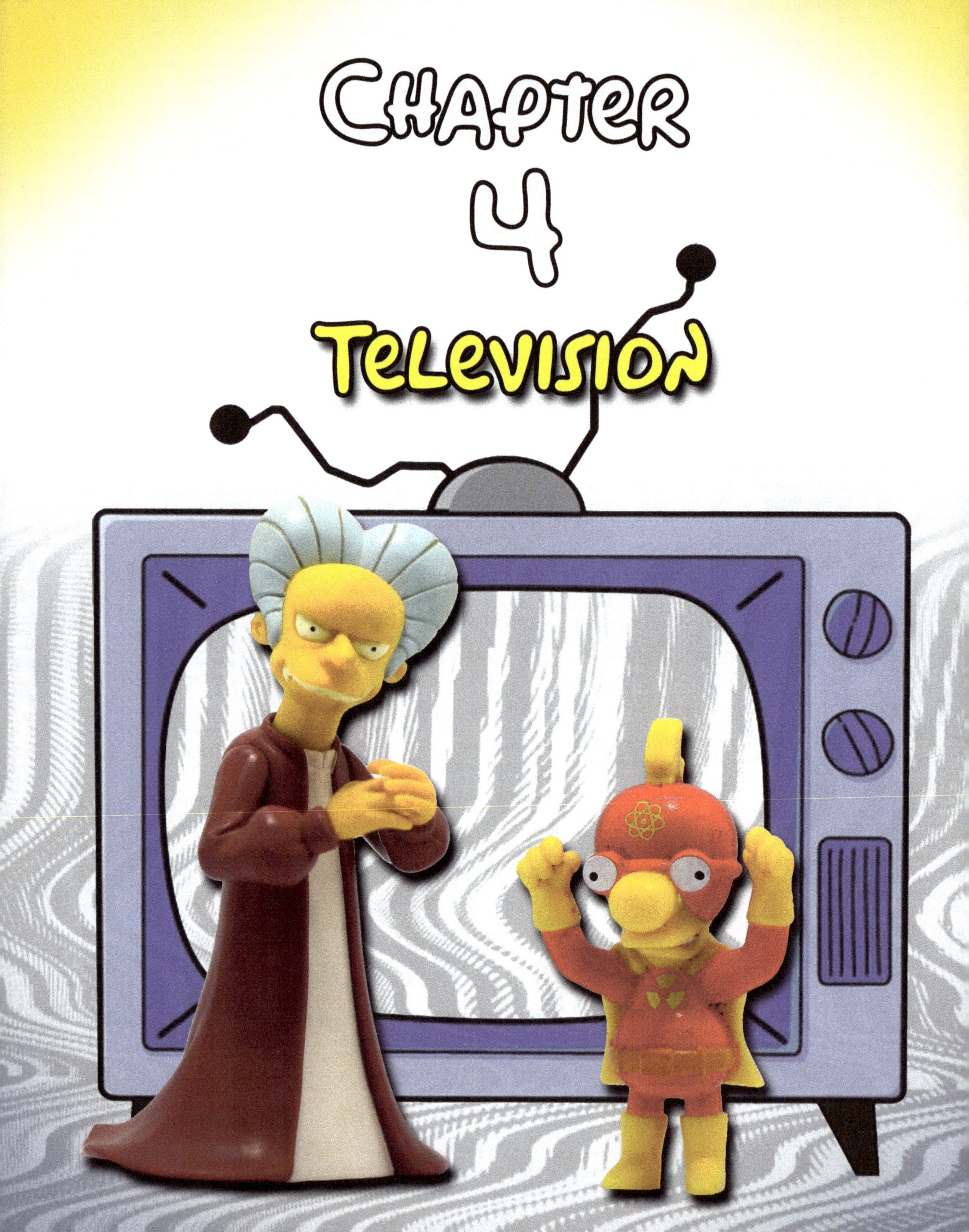
Chapter
4
Television

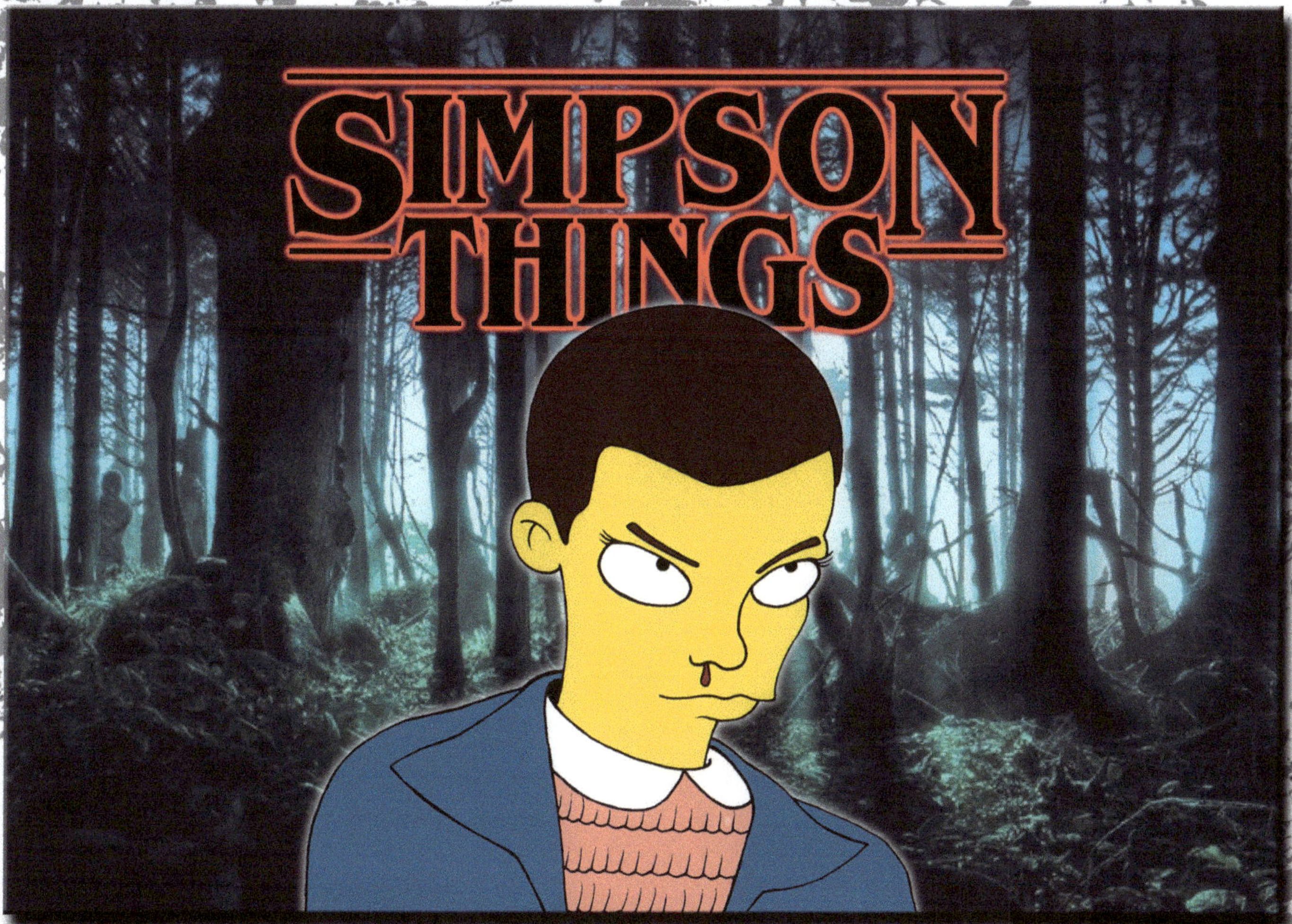

SIMPSON
THINGS

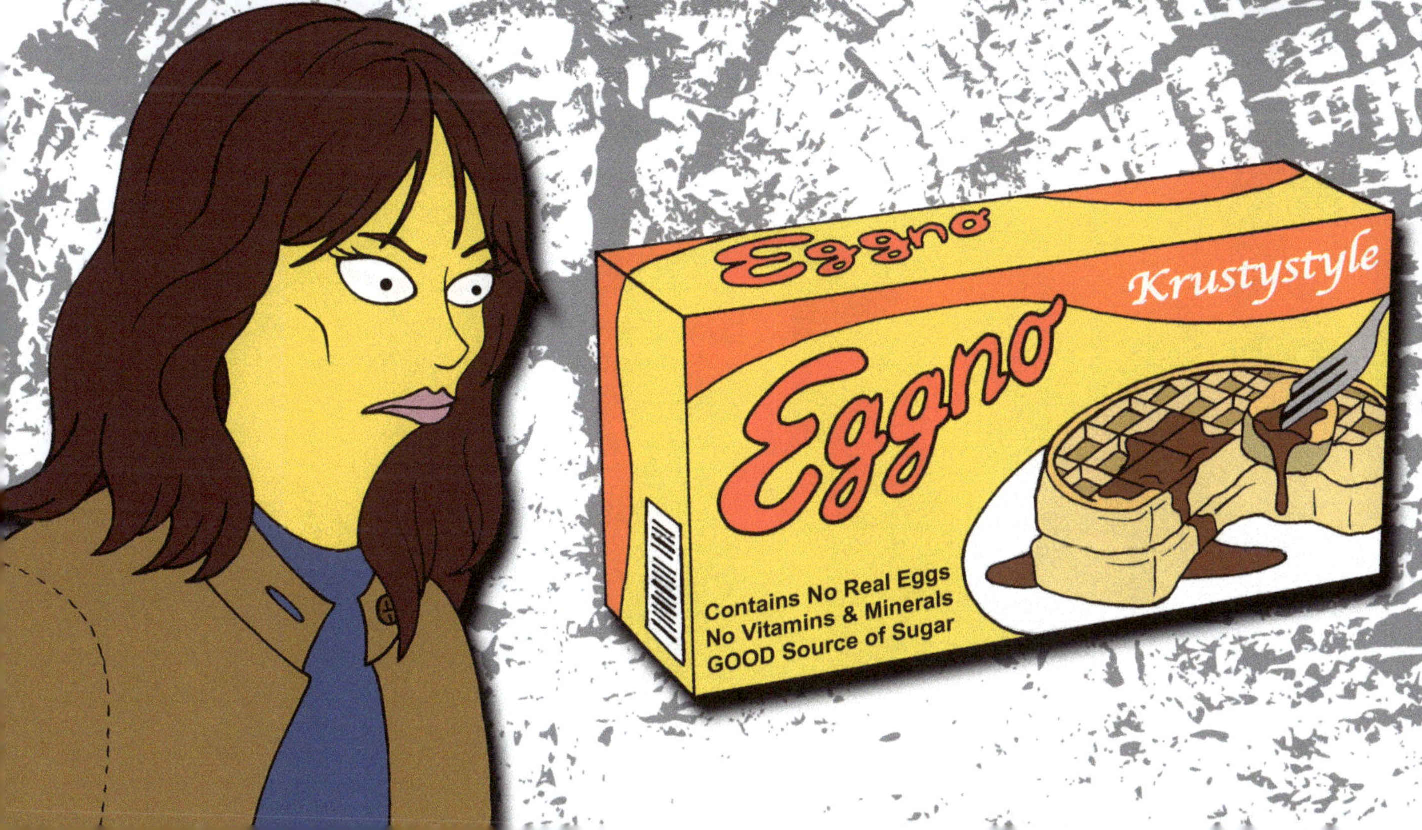

Eggno
Krustystyle
Eggno
Contains No Real Eggs
No Vitamins & Minerals
GOOD Source of Sugar

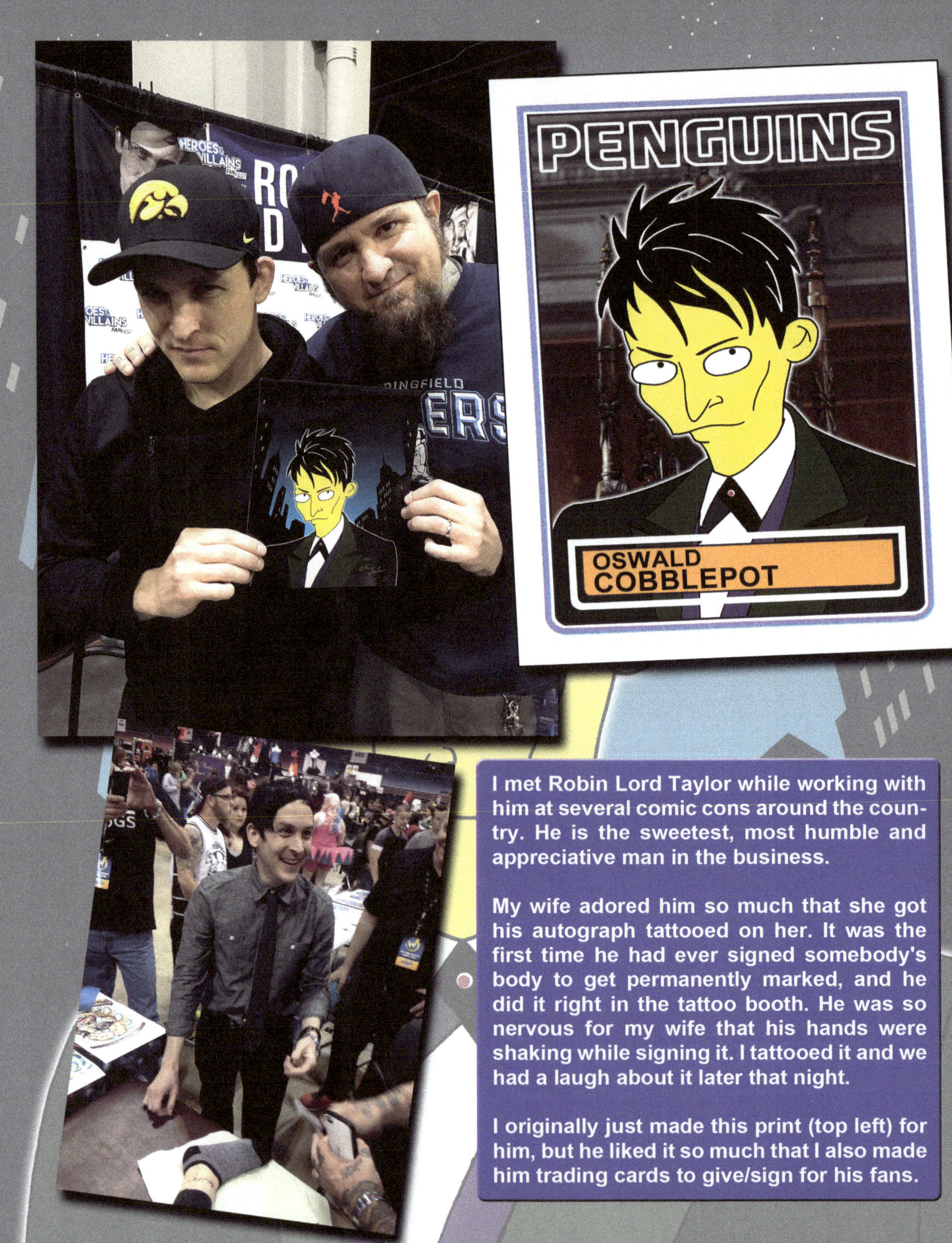

I met Robin Lord Taylor while working with him at several comic cons around the country. He is the sweetest, most humble and appreciative man in the business.

My wife adored him so much that she got his autograph tattooed on her. It was the first time he had ever signed somebody's body to get permanently marked, and he did it right in the tattoo booth. He was so nervous for my wife that his hands were shaking while signing it. I tattooed it and we had a laugh about it later that night.

I originally just made this print (top left) for him, but he liked it so much that I also made him trading cards to give/sign for his fans.

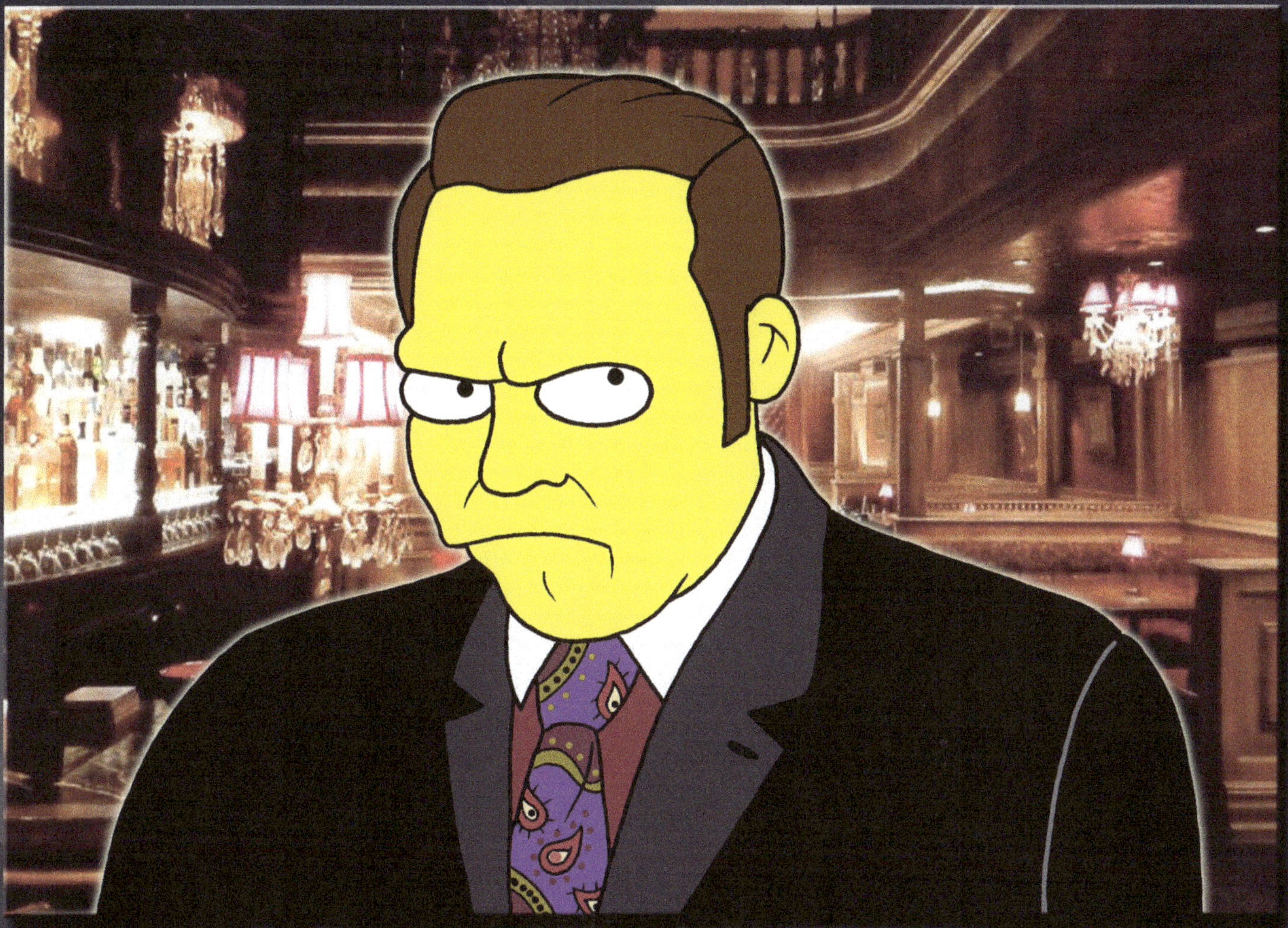

I have worked at dozens of entertainment conventions with Drew Powell, and I don't think I have ever seen a frown on the man's face. He is always laughing and joking around with both his peers and fans. He can be found playing acoustic guitar in the green room on his breaks, or throwing out first pitches at local ball games before the shows. Drew is a big Simpsons/Futurama fan, and bought this print from me (right) at the first convention we worked at together. As soon as I discovered his love for the Groening cartoons I made him his own version for his character *Butch* in Gotham.

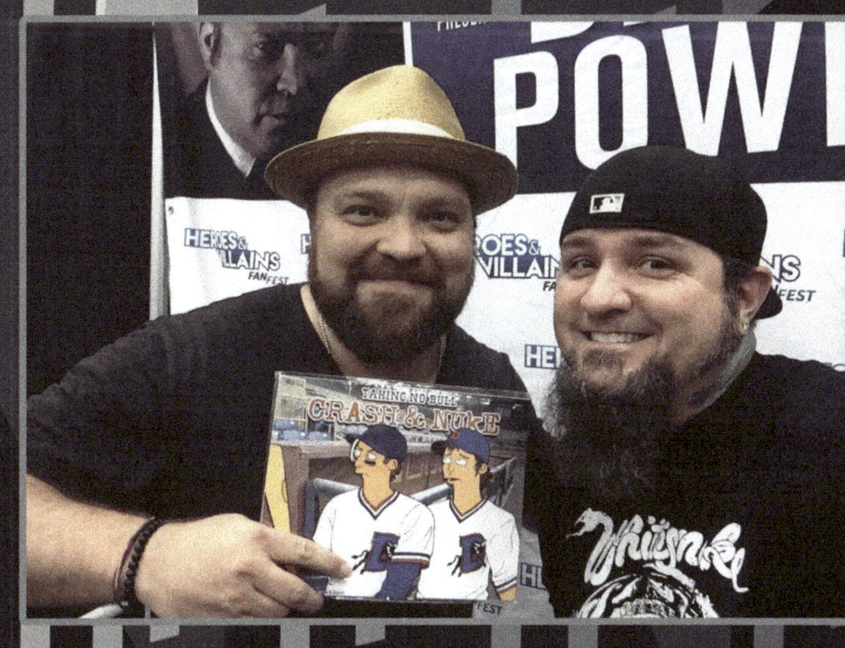

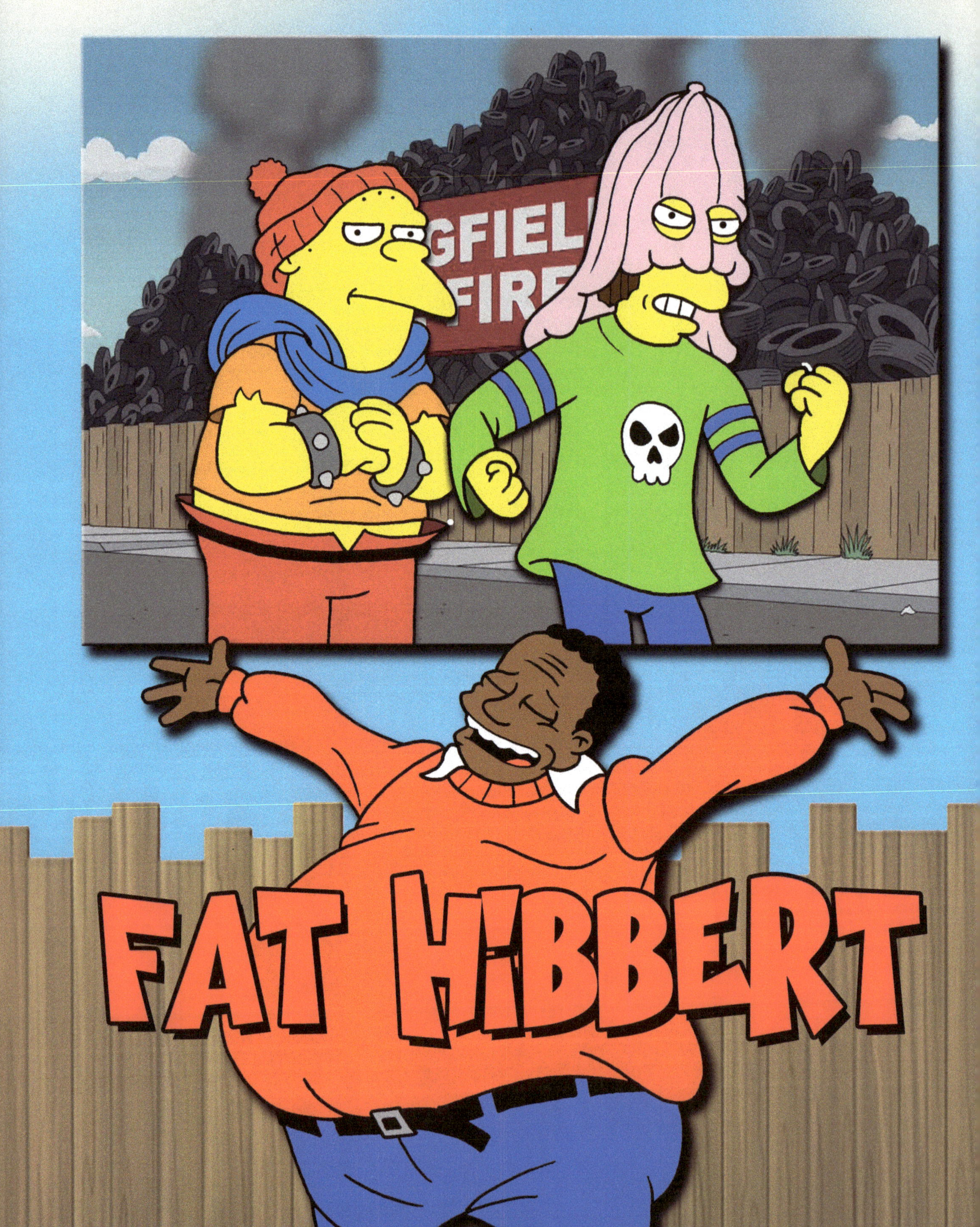
GFIEL
FIRE
FAT HIBBERT

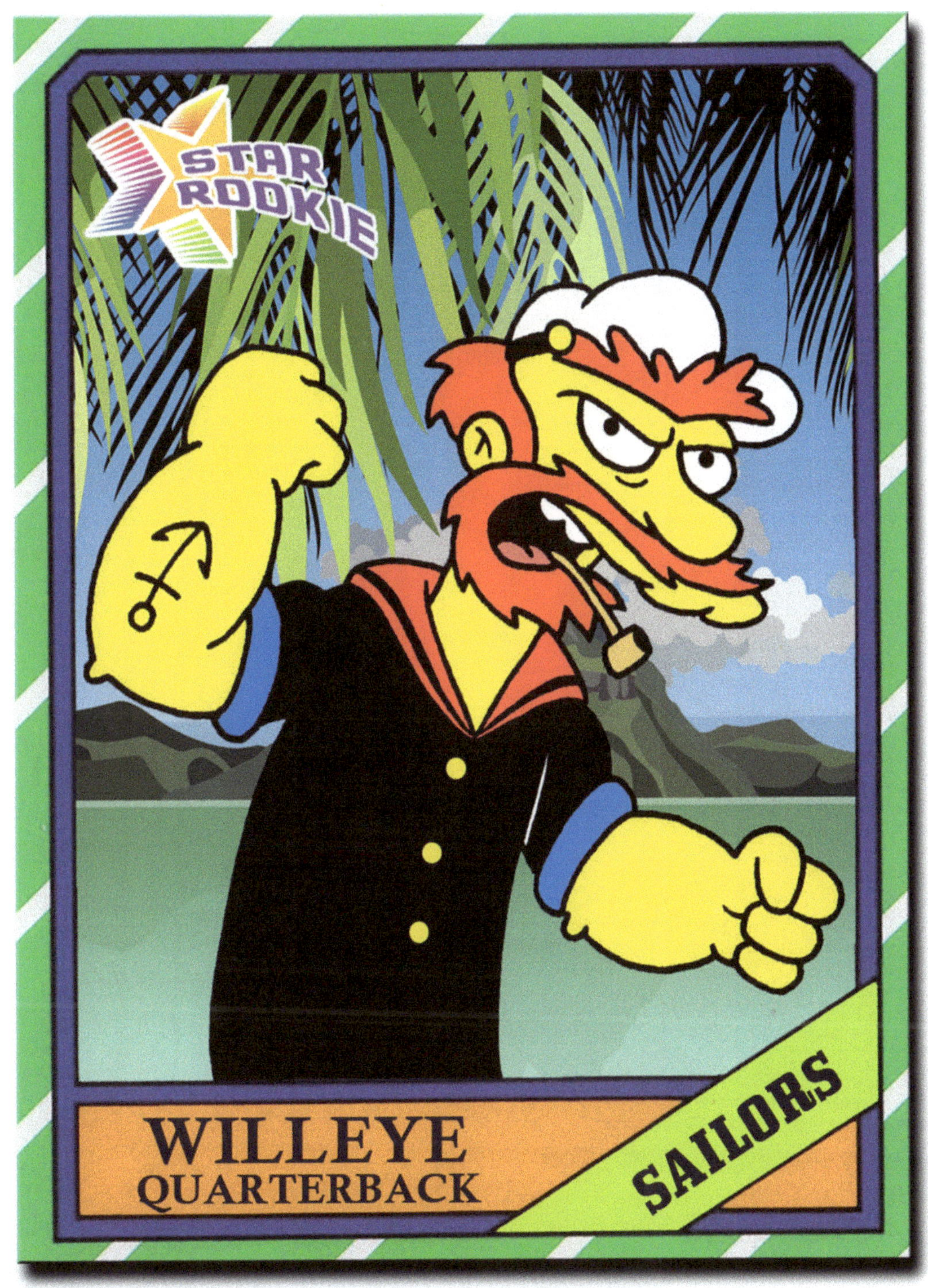

Sometimes you just see or hear similarities in characters, and no matter how hard you try you cannot dismiss them. Such was the case for me with Groundskeeper Willie and classic Popeye, so this weird creation came about pretty easily. I also mashed it up further and put it on an old 1986 football card to give it a theme, of what I'm not sure, but it was fun nonetheless.

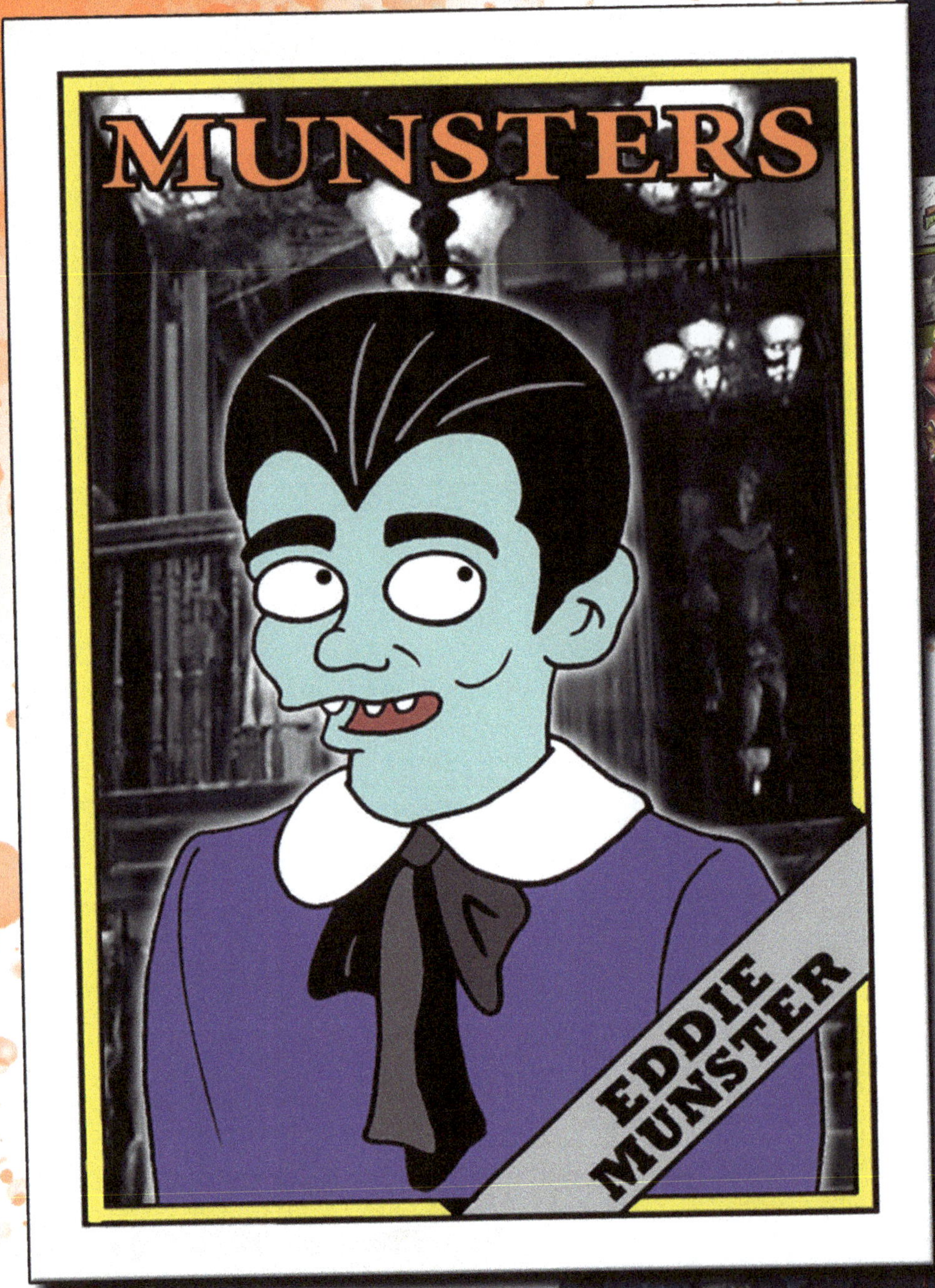

MUNSTERS

EDDIE MUNSTER

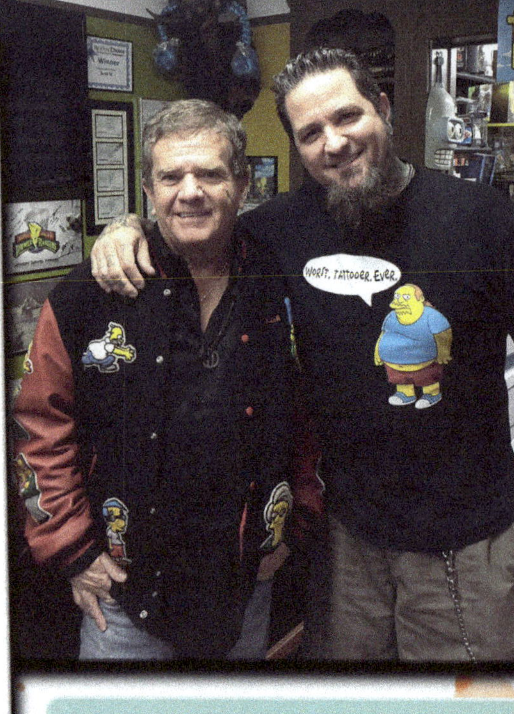

Butch stopped by my shop, Area 51 Tattoo in Springfield, OR. (above) in his official cast -issued Simpsons Jacket that he received for voicing his Munster's character on season 11, episode 8. (Below) I'm explaining my art, the "Simpsonsized" Eddie Munster in a yellow submarine to Butch. I tattooed it him on my show Epic Ink but unfortunately it got cut because of licensing issues

To me he's Uncle Butch. The iconic TV star has helped me in the entertainment business more than anyone. I often lean to him for advice or ideas, and he is always willing to attend my conventions or be involved in my projects, without question. I love Butch with all my heart.

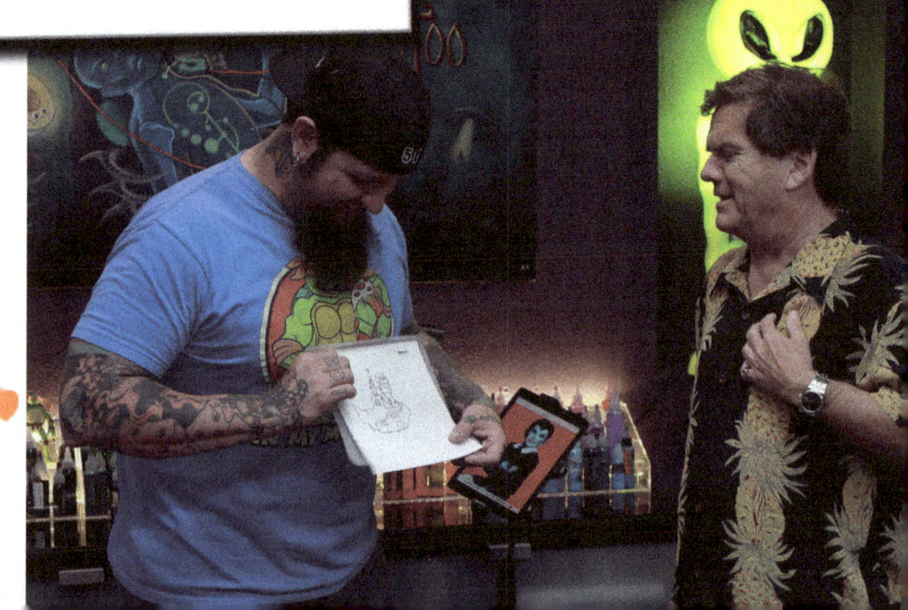

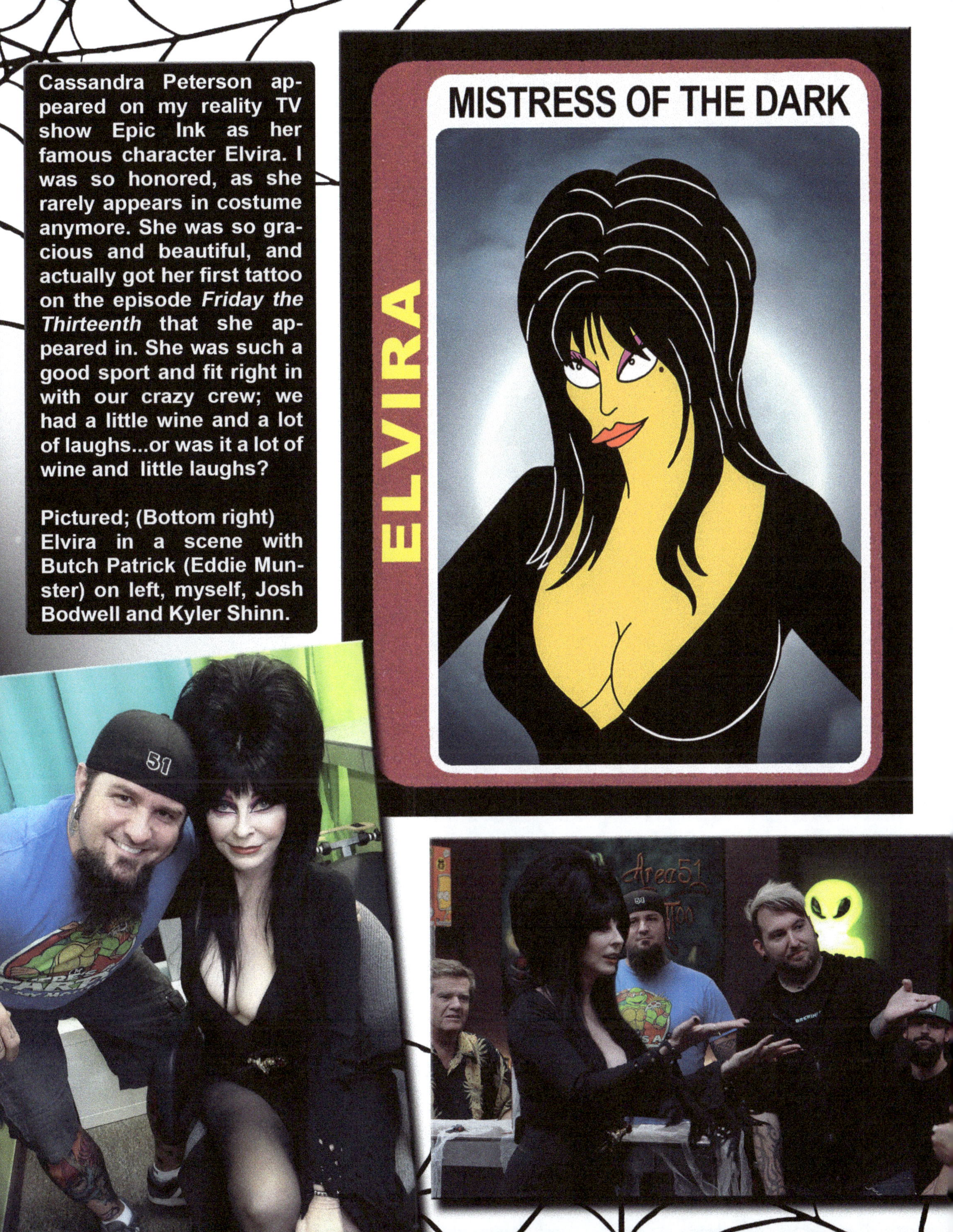

Cassandra Peterson appeared on my reality TV show Epic Ink as her famous character Elvira. I was so honored, as she rarely appears in costume anymore. She was so gracious and beautiful, and actually got her first tattoo on the episode *Friday the Thirteenth* that she appeared in. She was such a good sport and fit right in with our crazy crew; we had a little wine and a lot of laughs...or was it a lot of wine and little laughs?

Pictured; (Bottom right) Elvira in a scene with Butch Patrick (Eddie Munster) on left, myself, Josh Bodwell and Kyler Shinn.

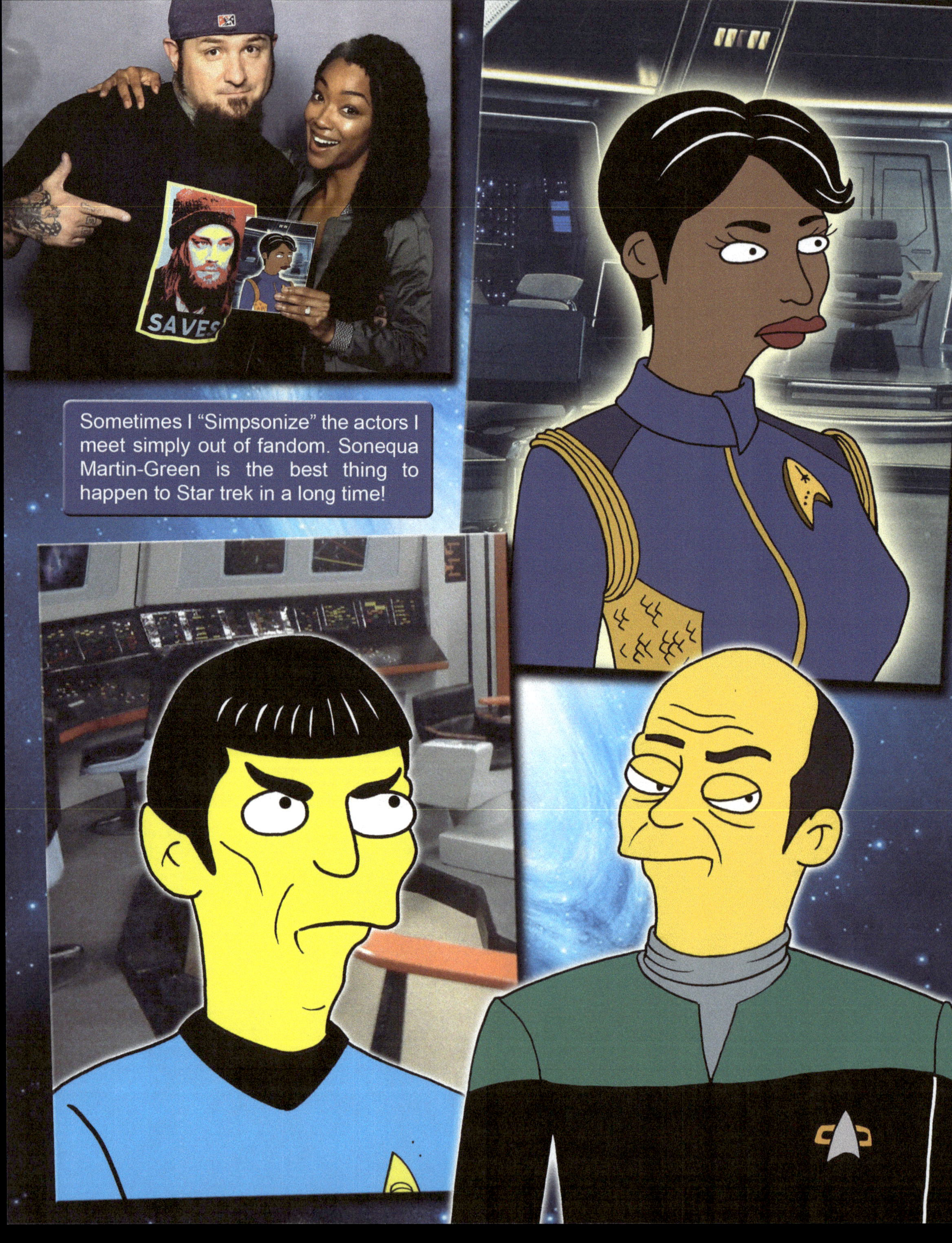

Sometimes I "Simpsonize" the actors I meet simply out of fandom. Sonequa Martin-Green is the best thing to happen to Star trek in a long time!

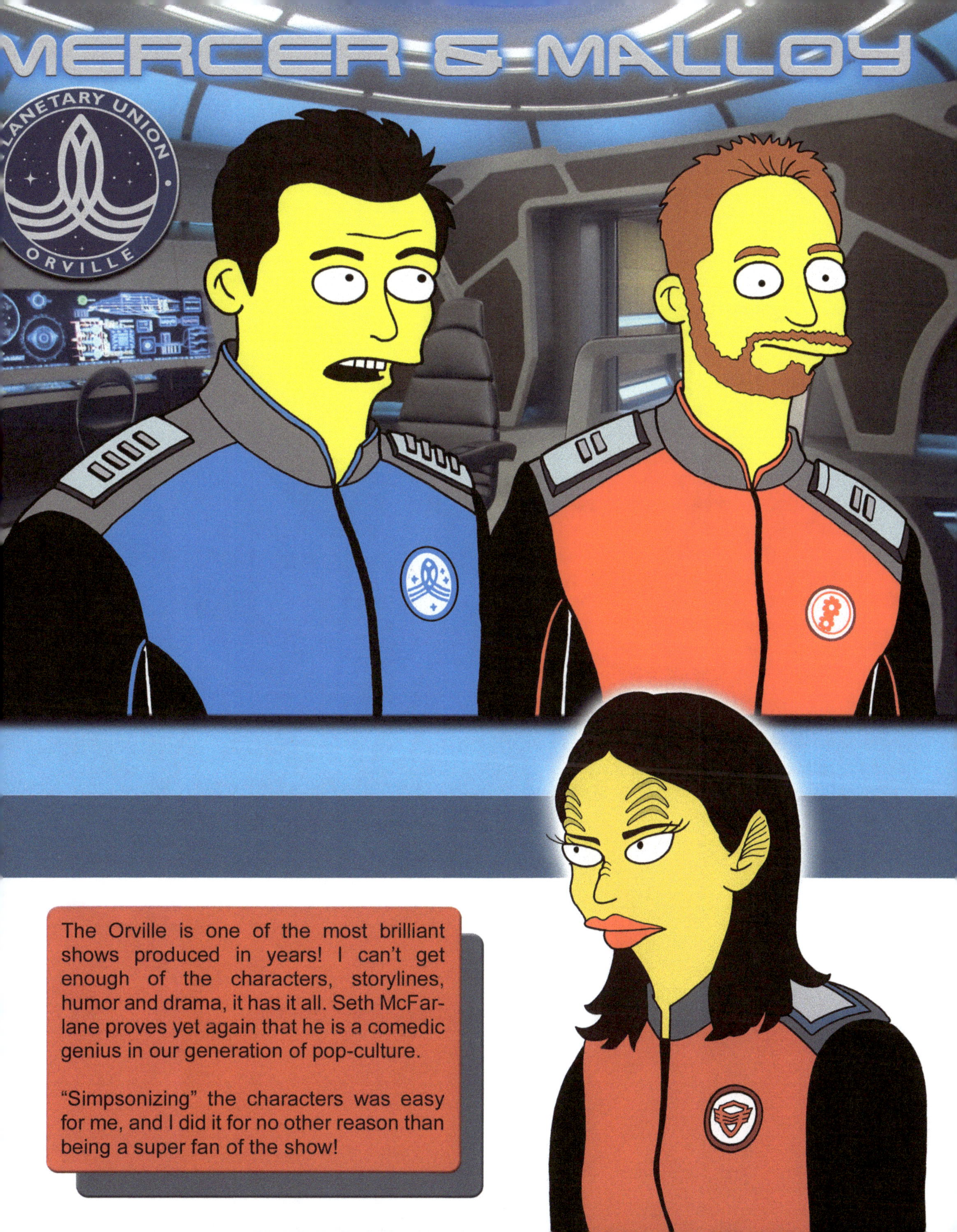
MERCER & MALLOY
LANETARY UNION
ORVILLE
The Orville is one of the most brilliant shows produced in years! I can't get enough of the characters, storylines, humor and drama, it has it all. Seth McFarlane proves yet again that he is a comedic genius in our generation of pop-culture.
"Simpsonizing" the characters was easy for me, and I did it for no other reason than being a super fan of the show!

Jon Bernthal may be The Punisher character on screen, but he's the most real man you'll ever meet in person. When his manager approached me and said, "Hey Jon heard you're the guy to get tattooed by, can you go talk to him about his idea?" *Sure*, I replied (shaking) and went straight over. "Yeah Chris, I want five tattoos...tonight, Jon answered with total confidence." So, I enlisted my good friend Kevin Becvar's help. We managed to get three done before he had to take off. Jon can come across as brash because of the characters he portrays, but when you get to know him you discover just how sweet and humble he is. He is respectful and thankful for everyone and everything around him. Jon asked about my kids and talked about his own. At our next event together my kids were with me and Jon blew their minds (and mine) when he stopped eating his lunch to come over and kneel down to their level to introduce himself, remembering their names and asking them about their grades and sports.

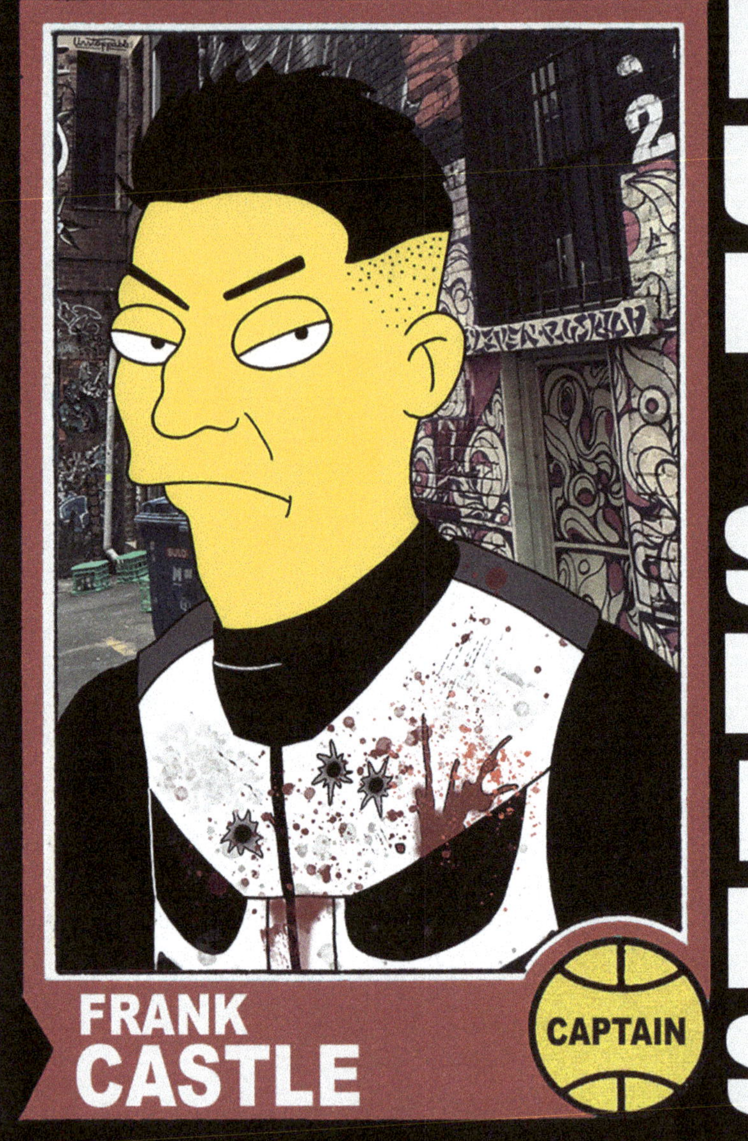

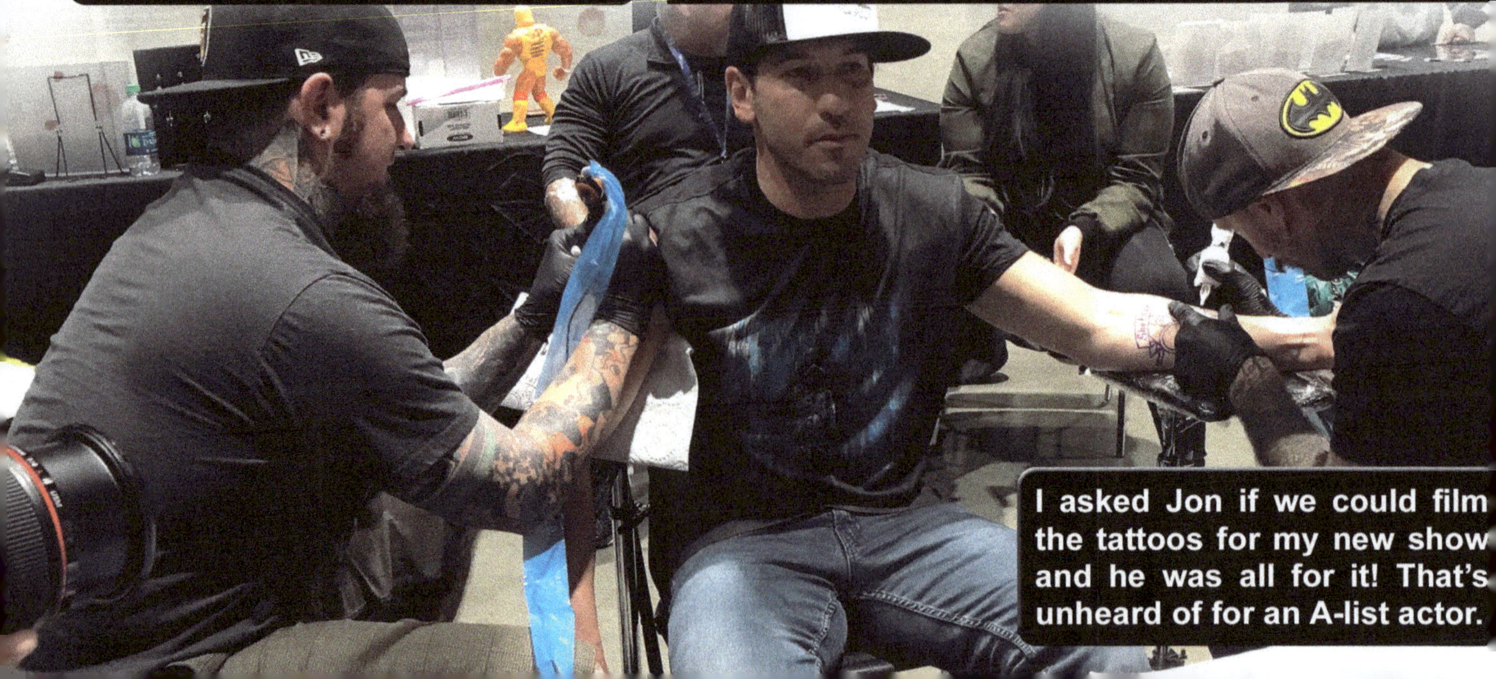

PUNISHERS

I asked Jon if we could film the tattoos for my new show and he was all for it! That's unheard of for an A-list actor.

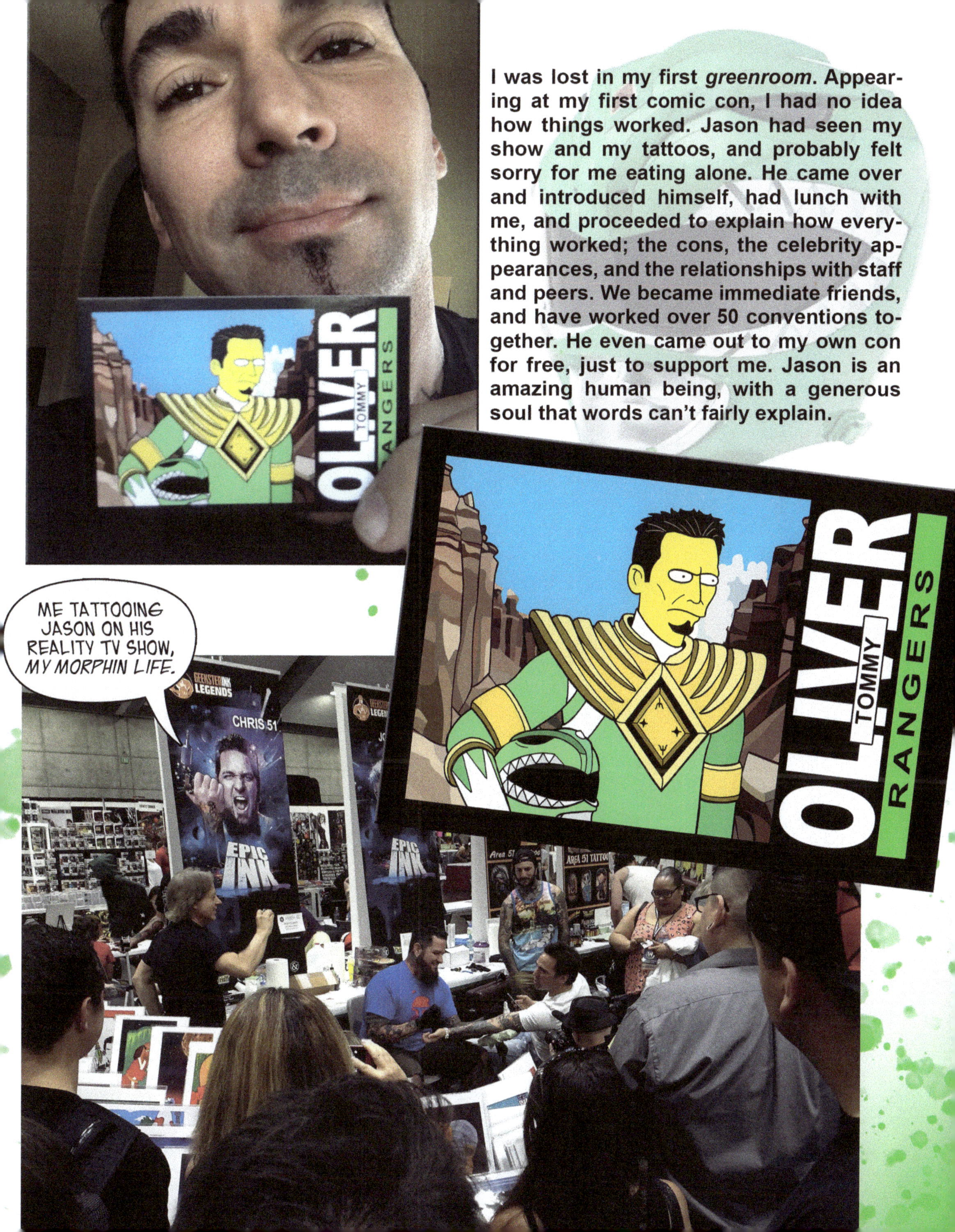

I was lost in my first *greenroom*. Appearing at my first comic con, I had no idea how things worked. Jason had seen my show and my tattoos, and probably felt sorry for me eating alone. He came over and introduced himself, had lunch with me, and proceeded to explain how everything worked; the cons, the celebrity appearances, and the relationships with staff and peers. We became immediate friends, and have worked over 50 conventions together. He even came out to my own con for free, just to support me. Jason is an amazing human being, with a generous soul that words can't fairly explain.

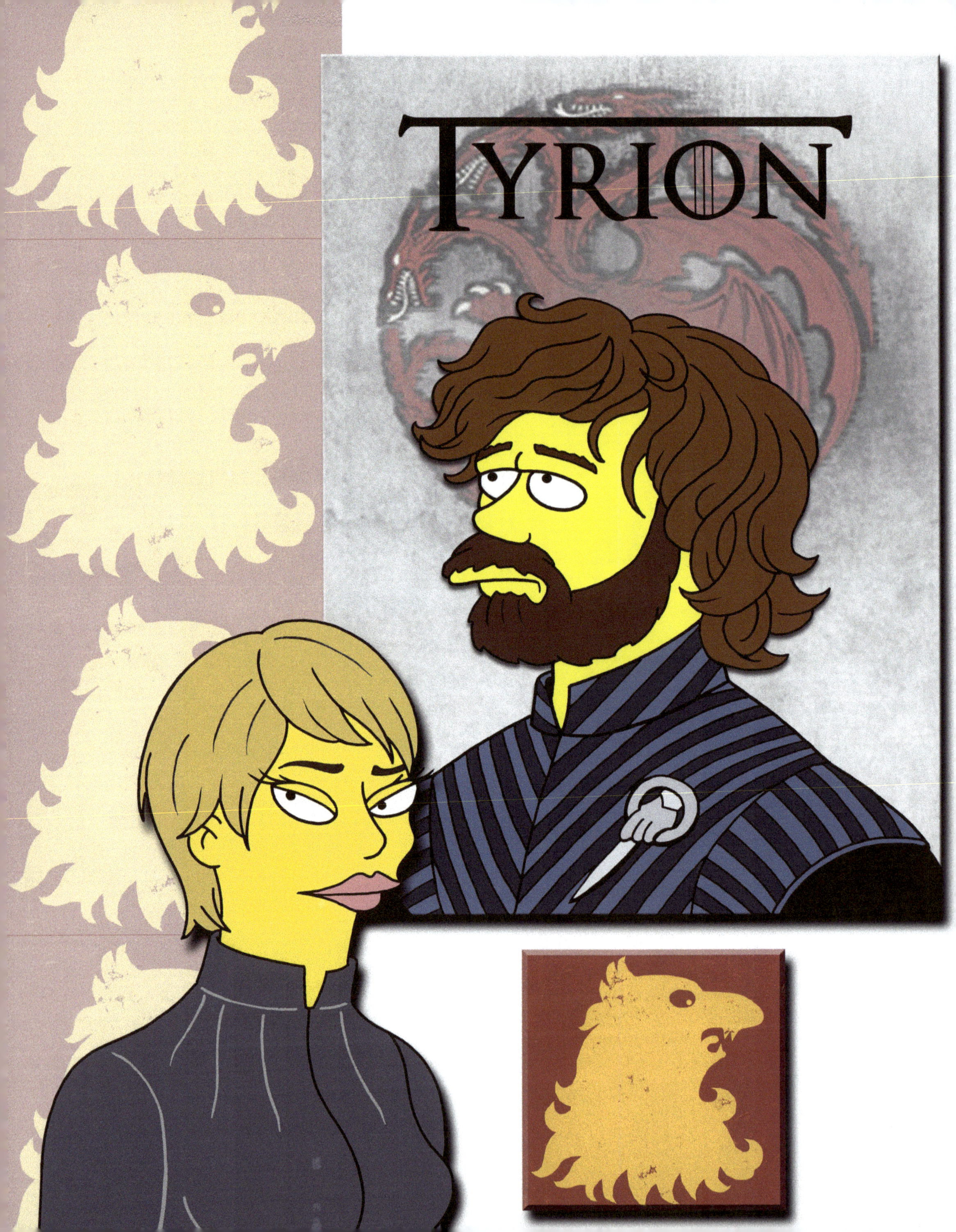
TYRION

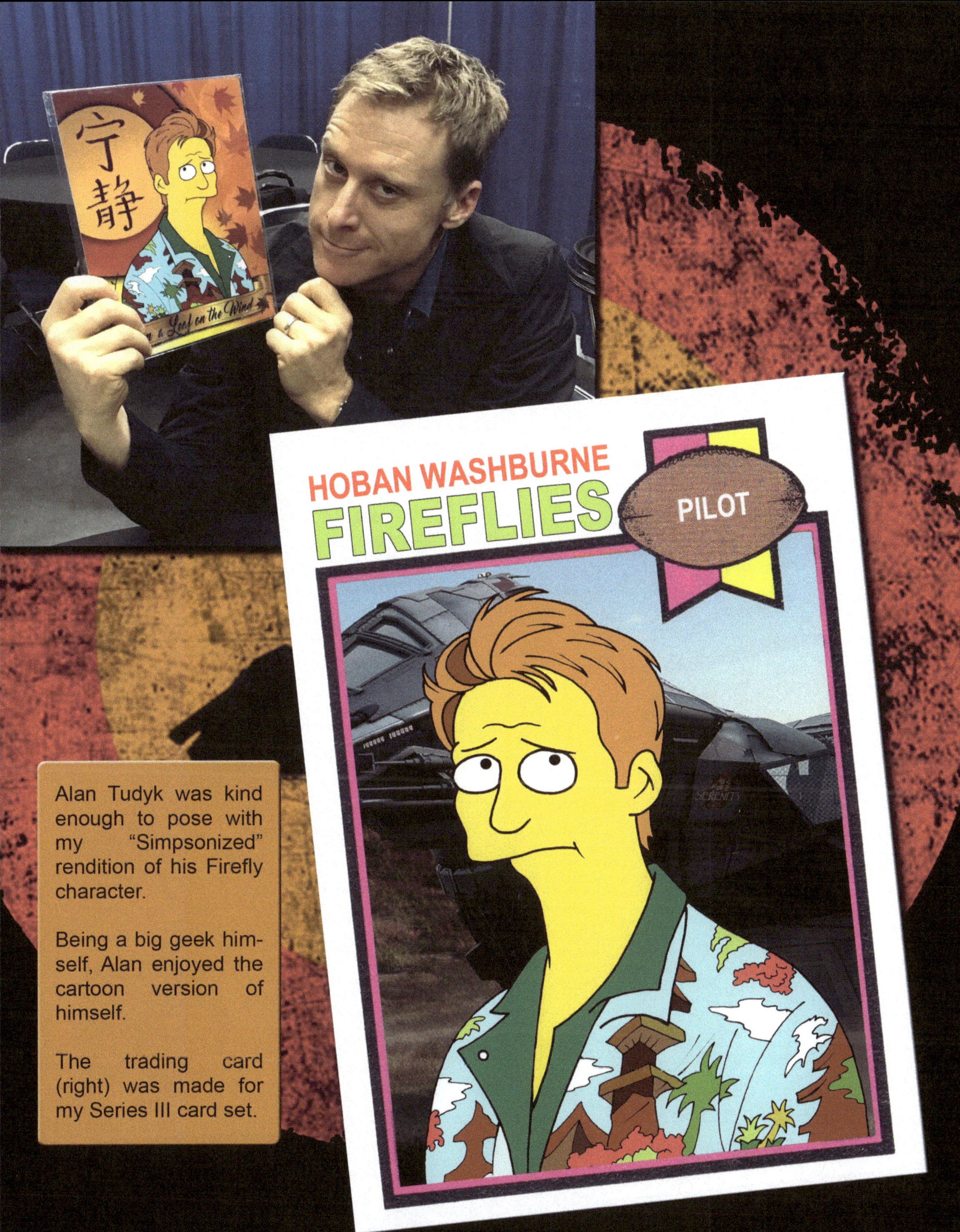

Alan Tudyk was kind enough to pose with my "Simpsonized" rendition of his Firefly character.

Being a big geek himself, Alan enjoyed the cartoon version of himself.

The trading card (right) was made for my Series III card set.

Chapter 5

Sport Balls

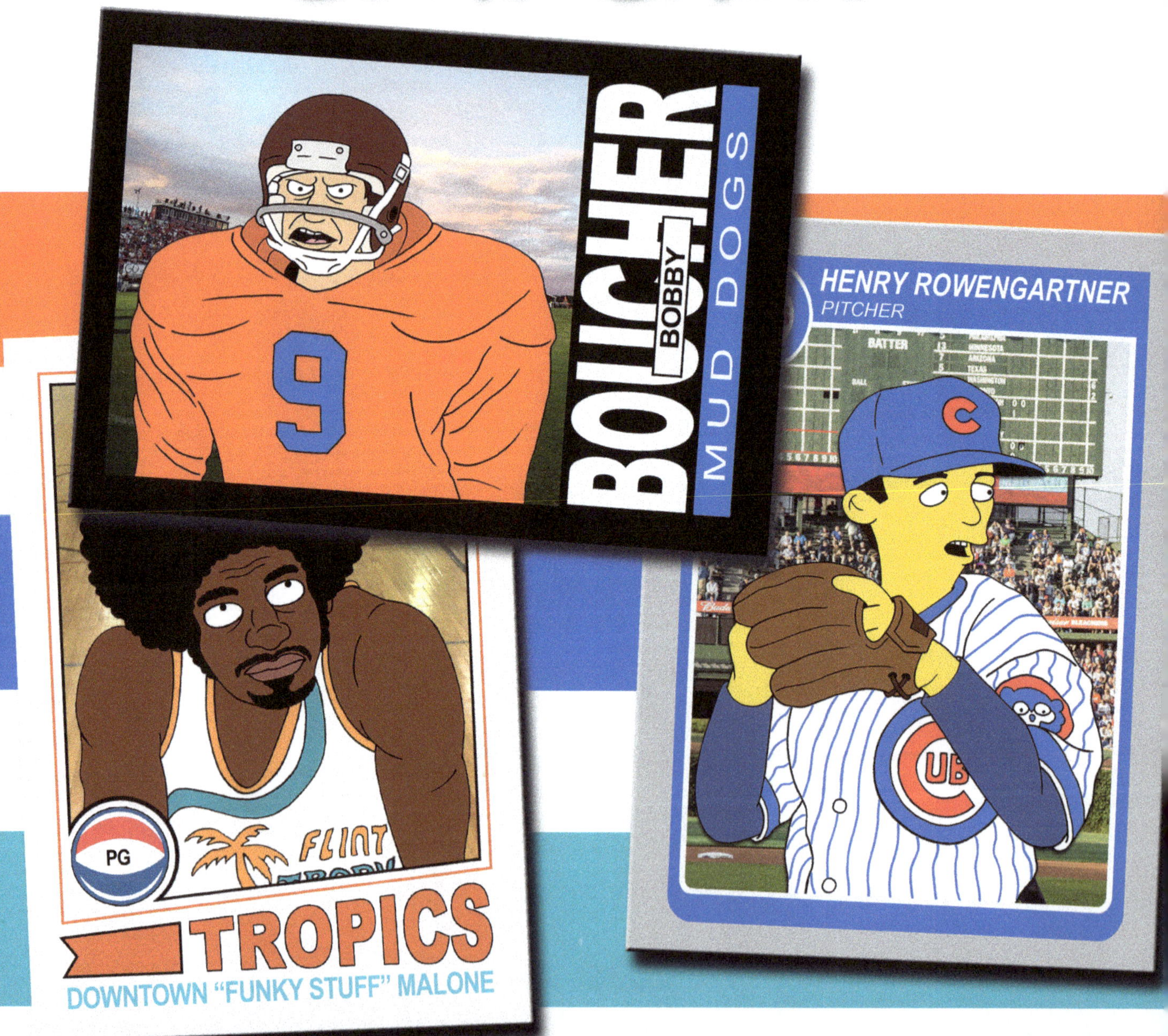

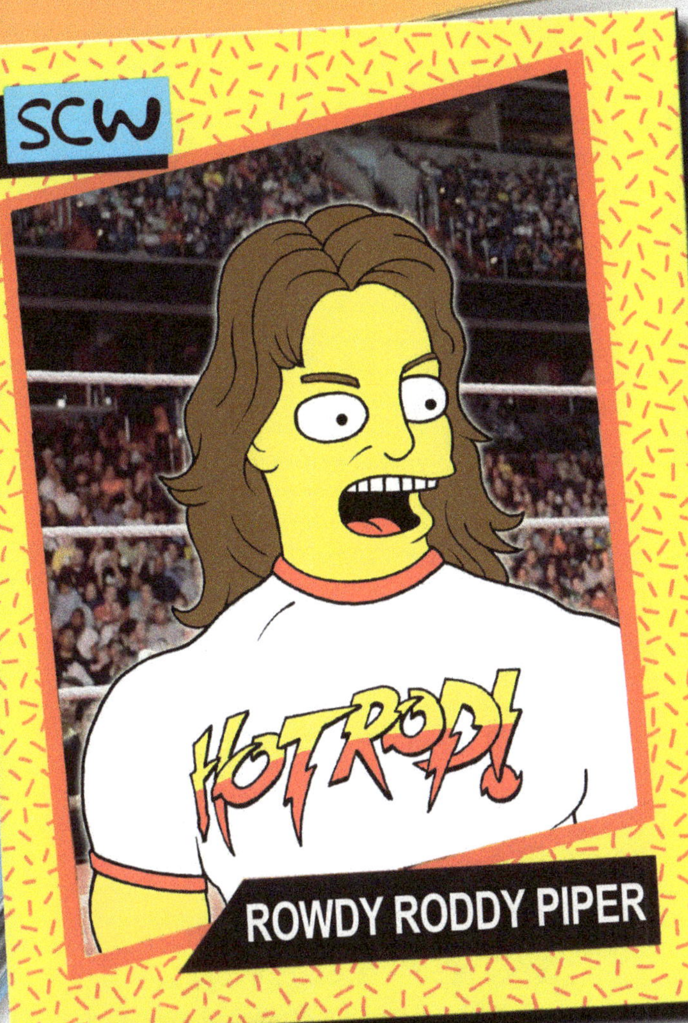
SCW
HOT ROD!
ROWDY RODDY PIPER

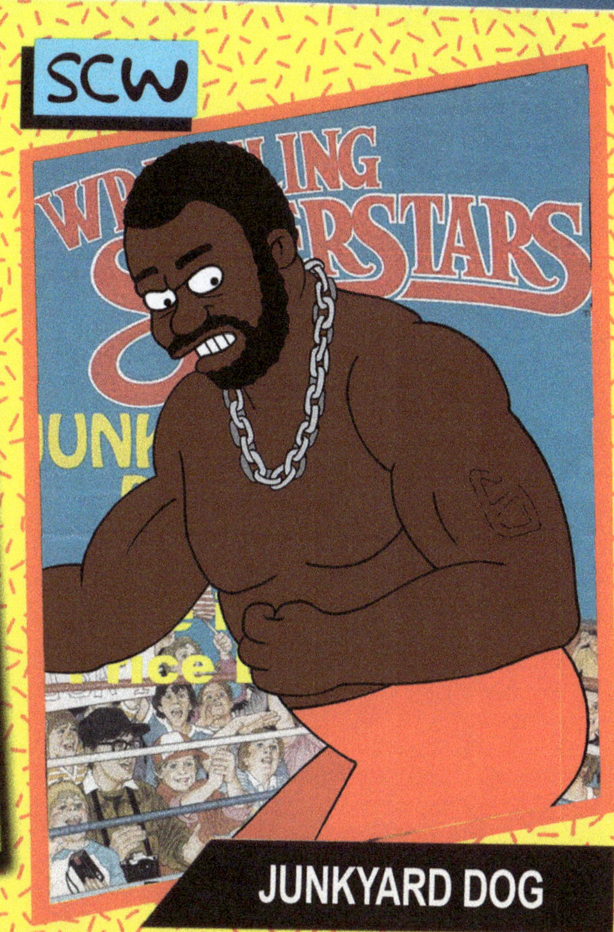
SCW
JUNKYARD DOG

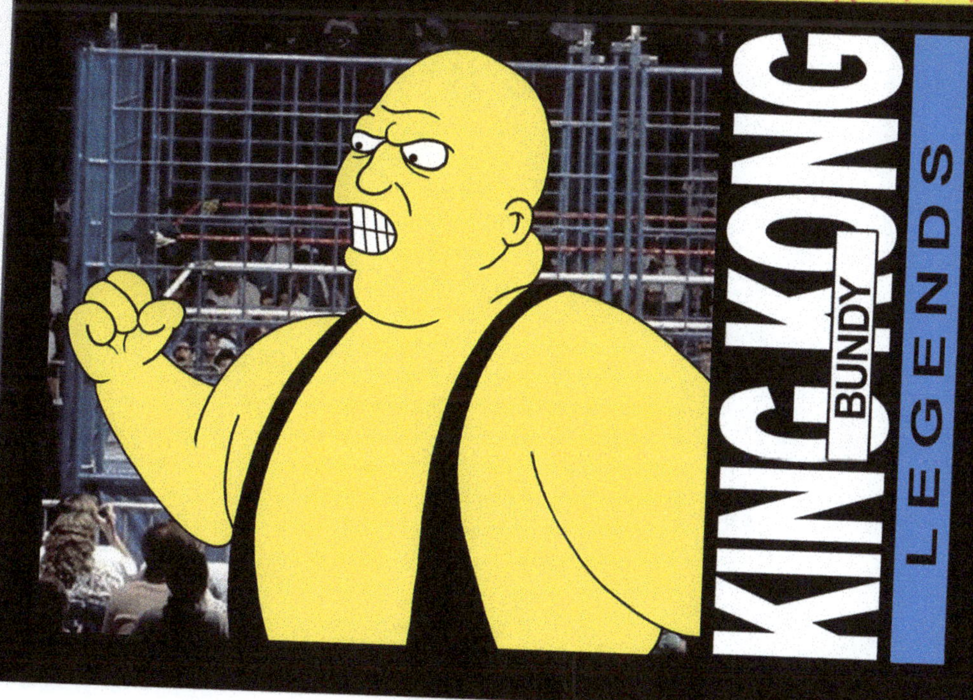
KING KONG
BUNDY
LEGENDS

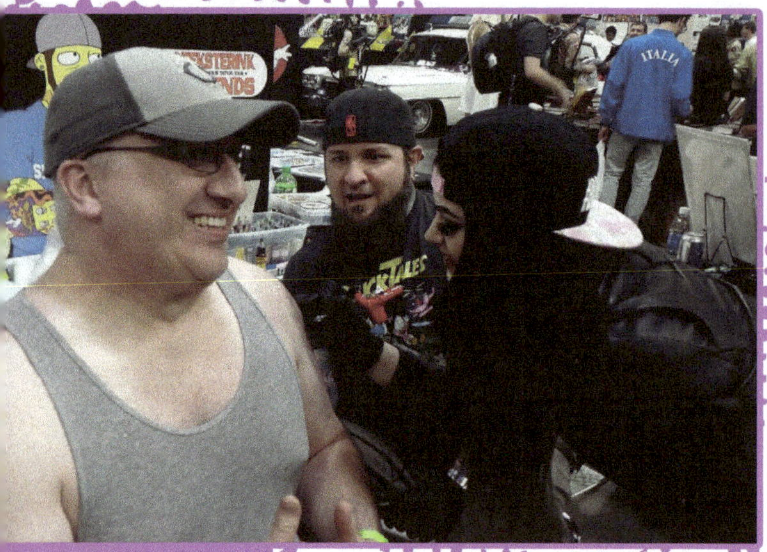

(Above) Just for fun, Paige grabbed my tattoo machine and pretended to take over on my client, who was a huge fan of hers. (Below) Saraya visiting my shop, Area 51, to get tattooed while in town for a WWE event

WWE Diva Paige is one of the most real, down to earth people I have ever met. She would regularly visit my tattoo booth at conventions we were both working, and through the ink we became friends. She really connected with my wife, and whenever WWE comes around she calls us to come watch the event, not the other way around. I have personally seen her spend so much of her own time connecting with so many young girls and fans, always giving positive support and advice. She deserves all the fame & fortune coming her way, because nobody has worked harder.

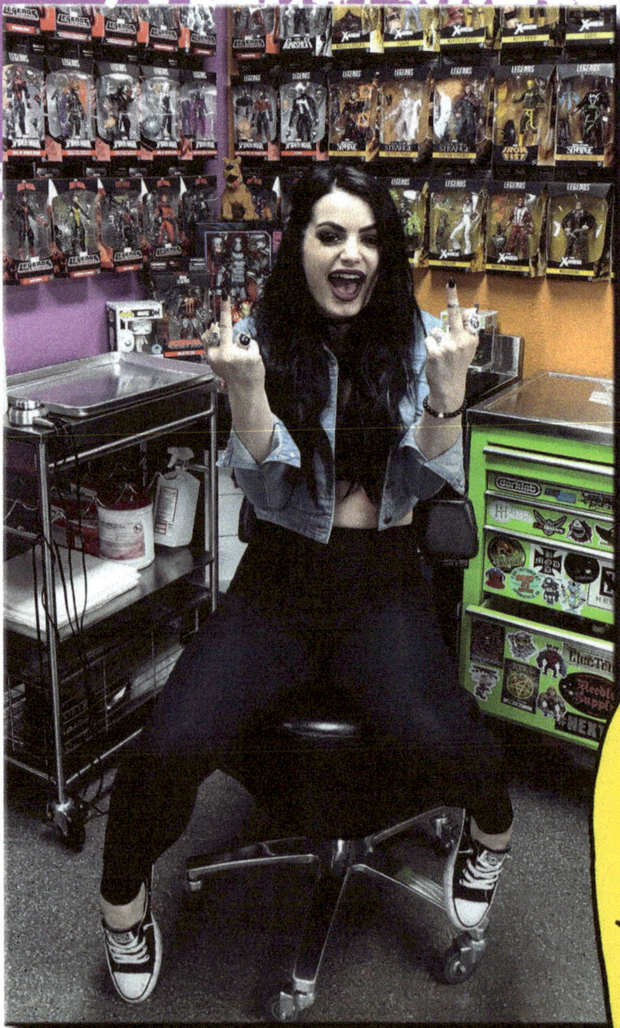

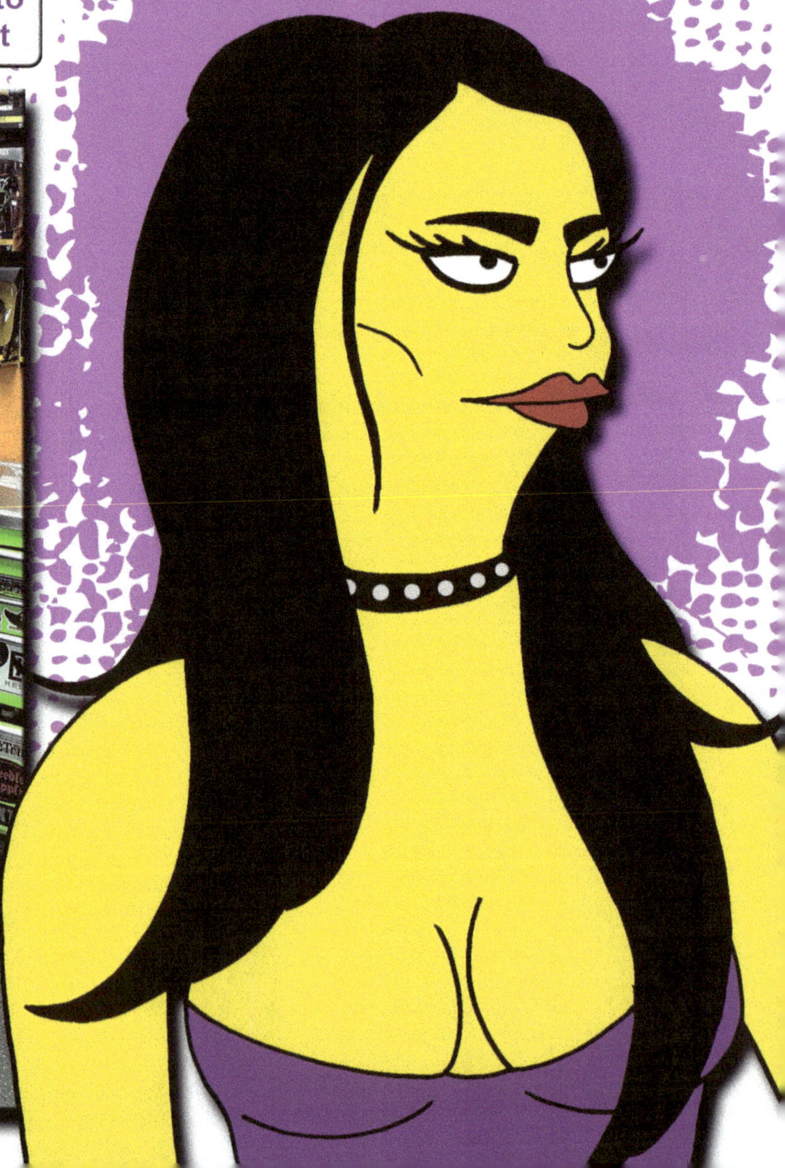

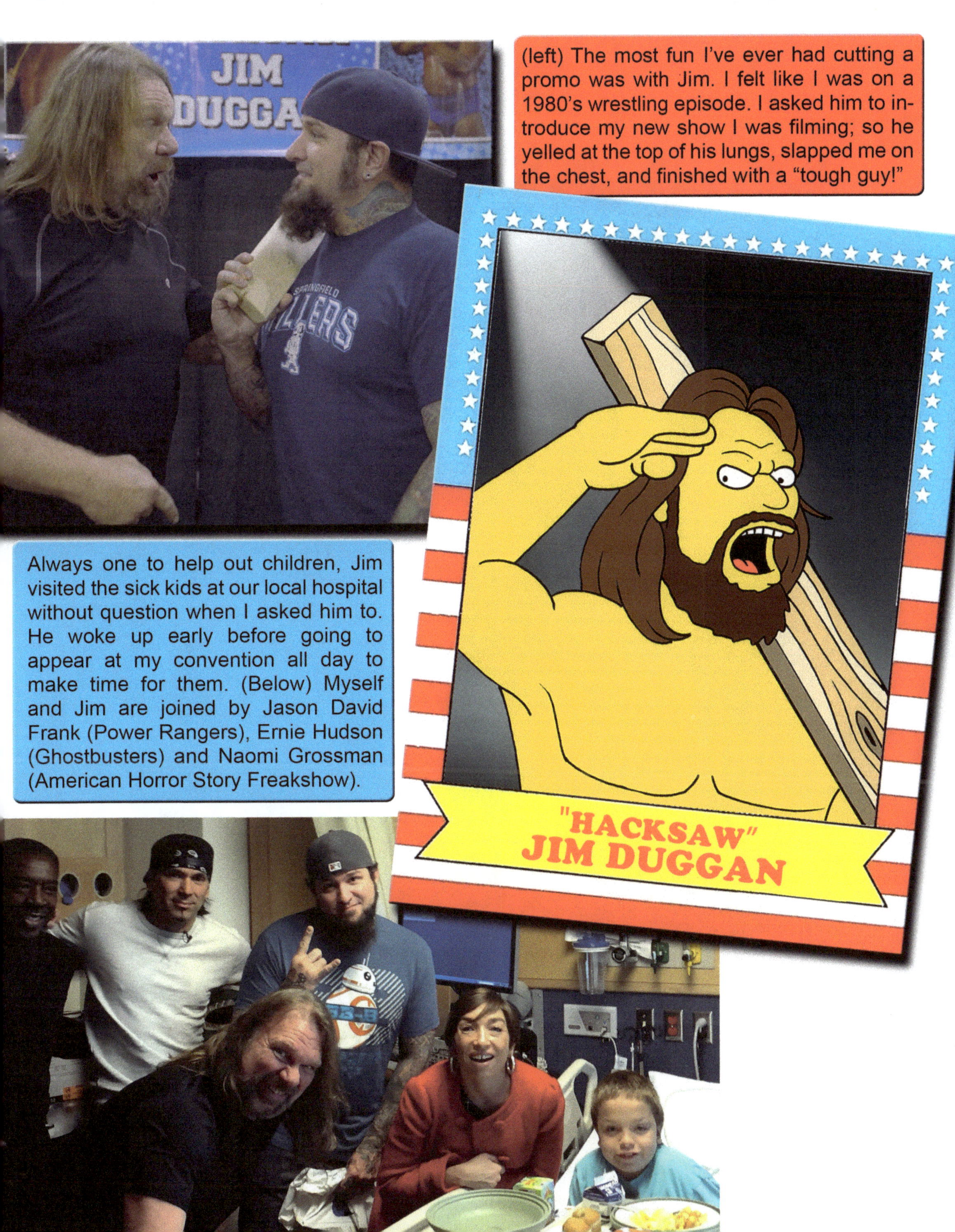

(left) The most fun I've ever had cutting a promo was with Jim. I felt like I was on a 1980's wrestling episode. I asked him to introduce my new show I was filming; so he yelled at the top of his lungs, slapped me on the chest, and finished with a "tough guy!"

Always one to help out children, Jim visited the sick kids at our local hospital without question when I asked him to. He woke up early before going to appear at my convention all day to make time for them. (Below) Myself and Jim are joined by Jason David Frank (Power Rangers), Ernie Hudson (Ghostbusters) and Naomi Grossman (American Horror Story Freakshow).

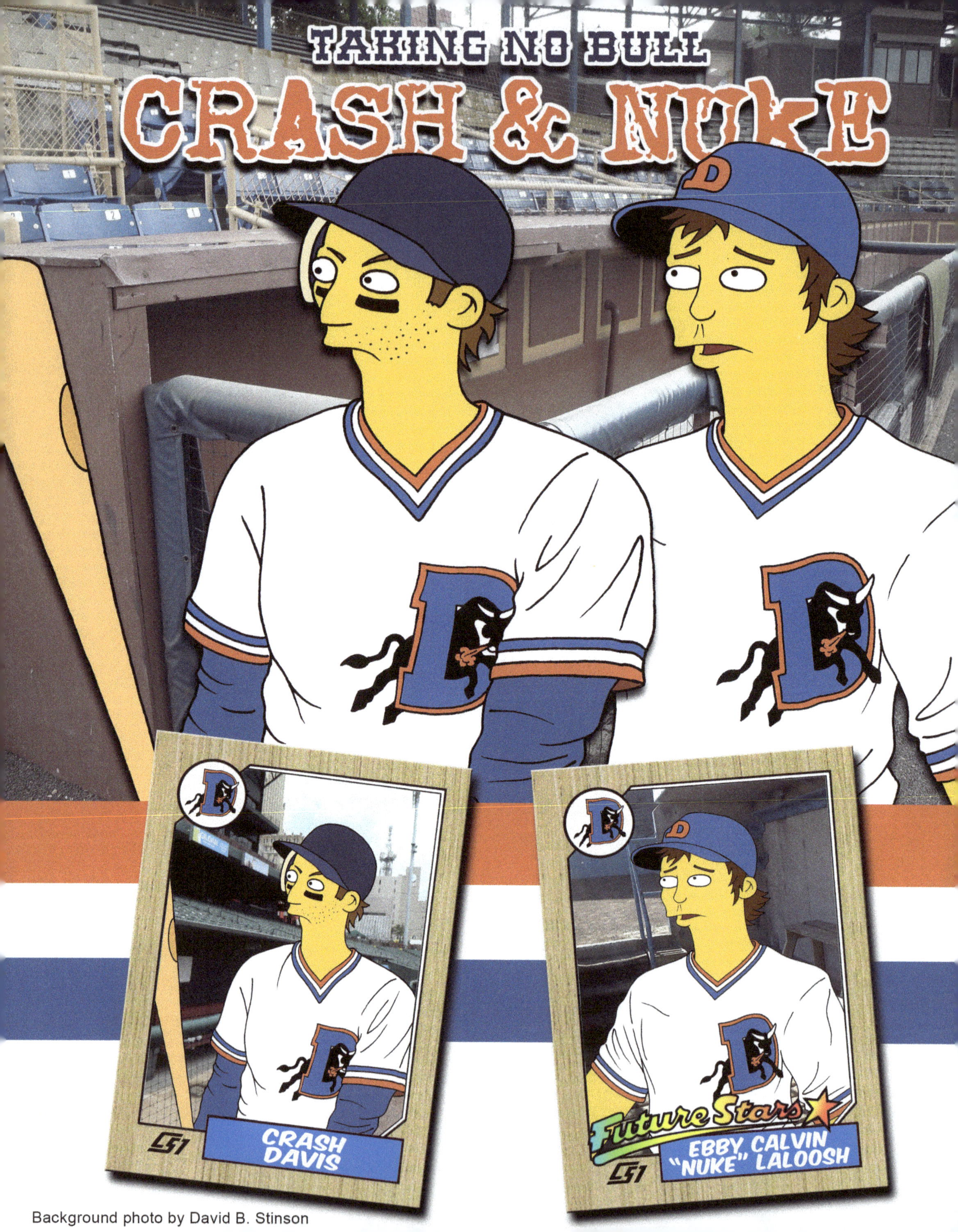

Background photo by David B. Stinson

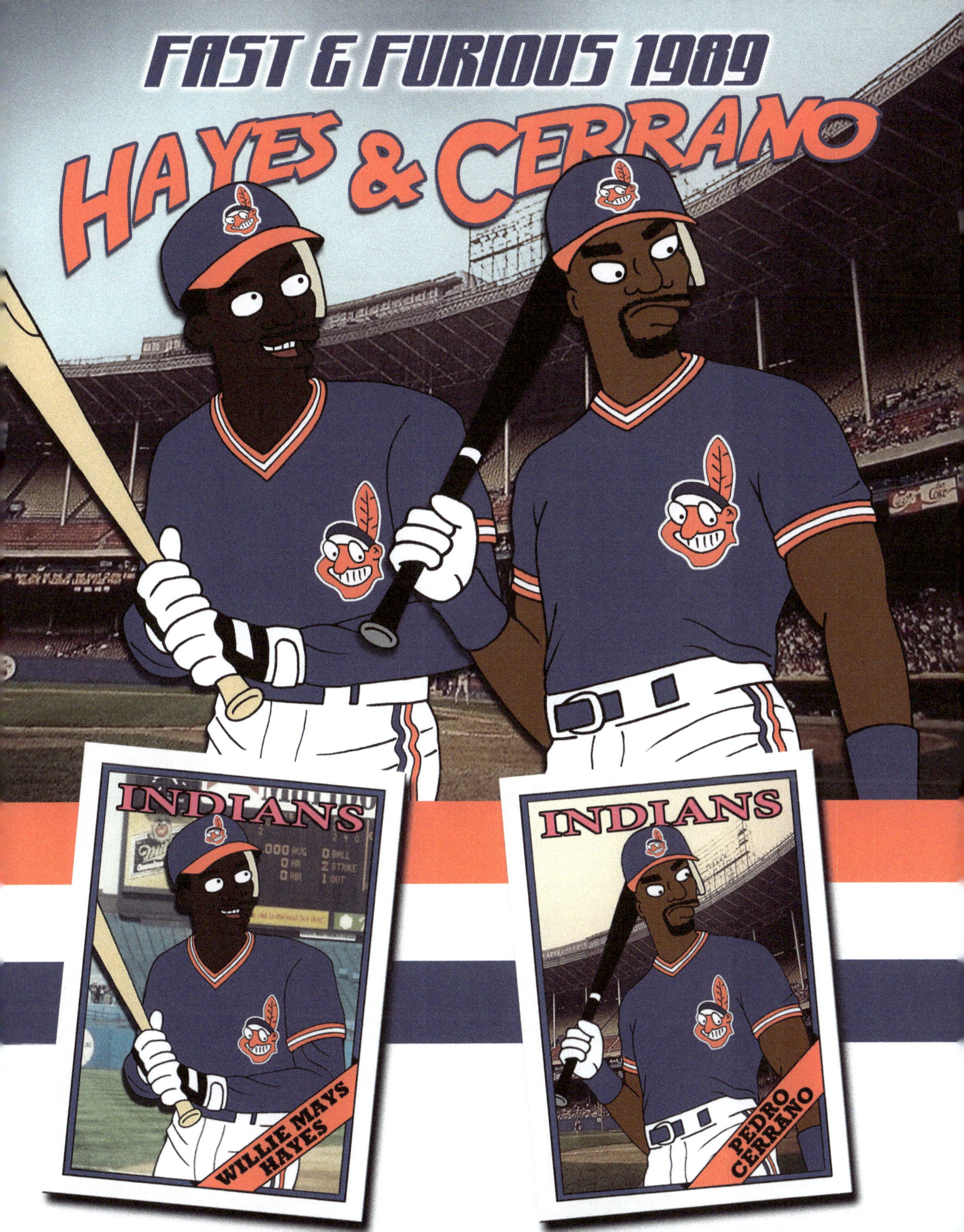
FAST & FURIOUS 1989
HAYES & CERRANO
INDIANS
WILLIE MAYS HAYES
INDIANS
PEDRO CERRANO

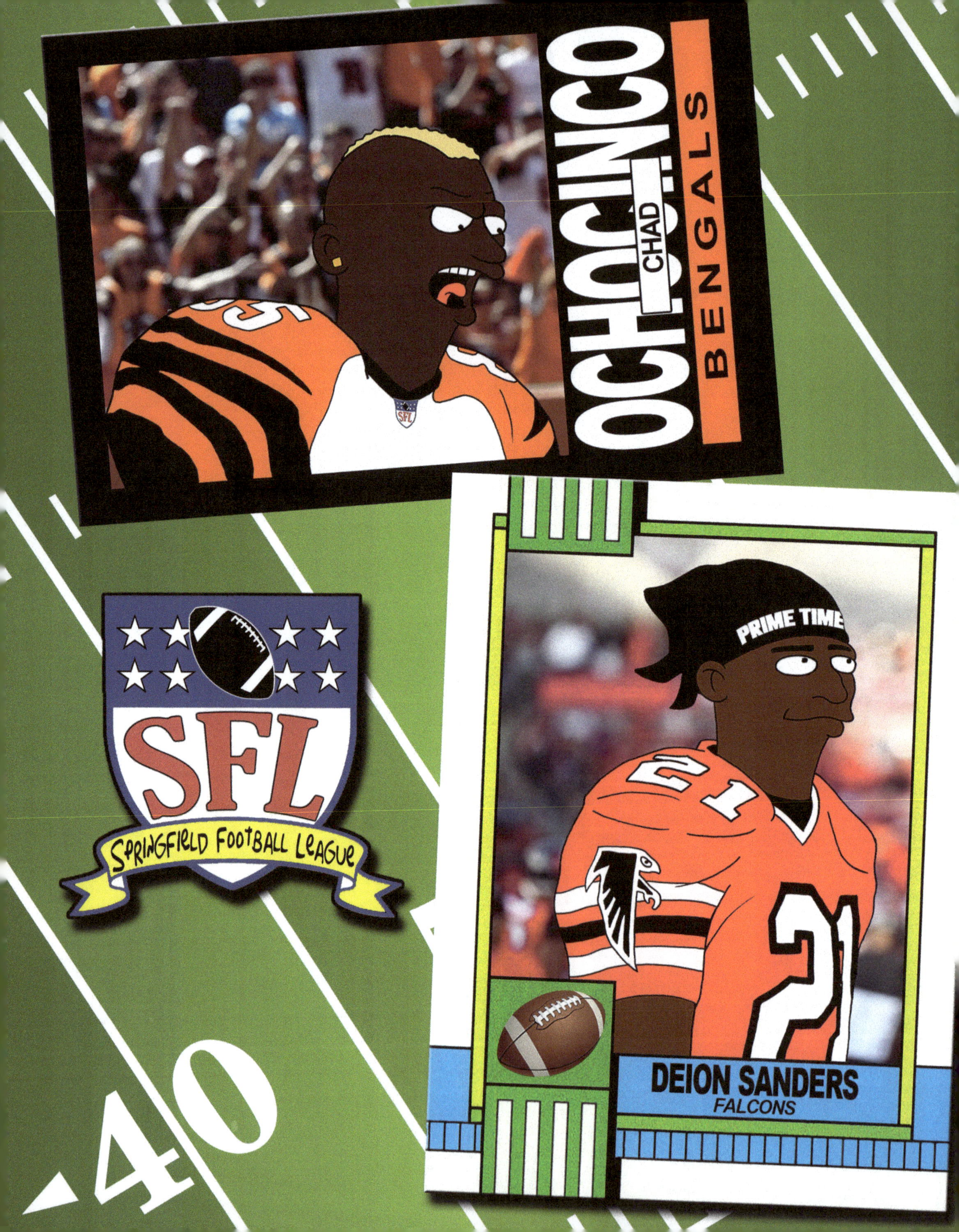

CHAD
OCHOCINCO
BENGALS

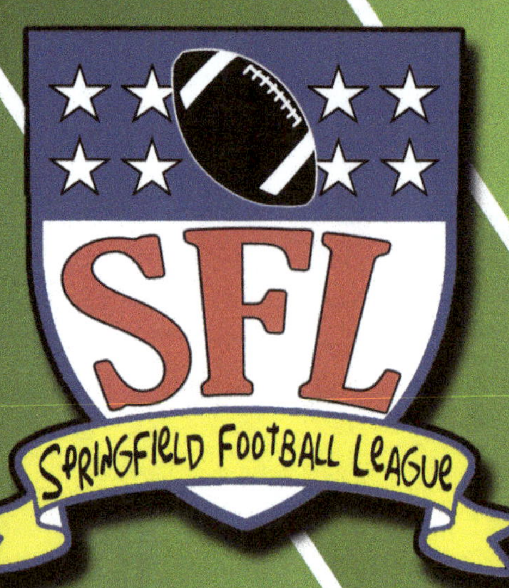

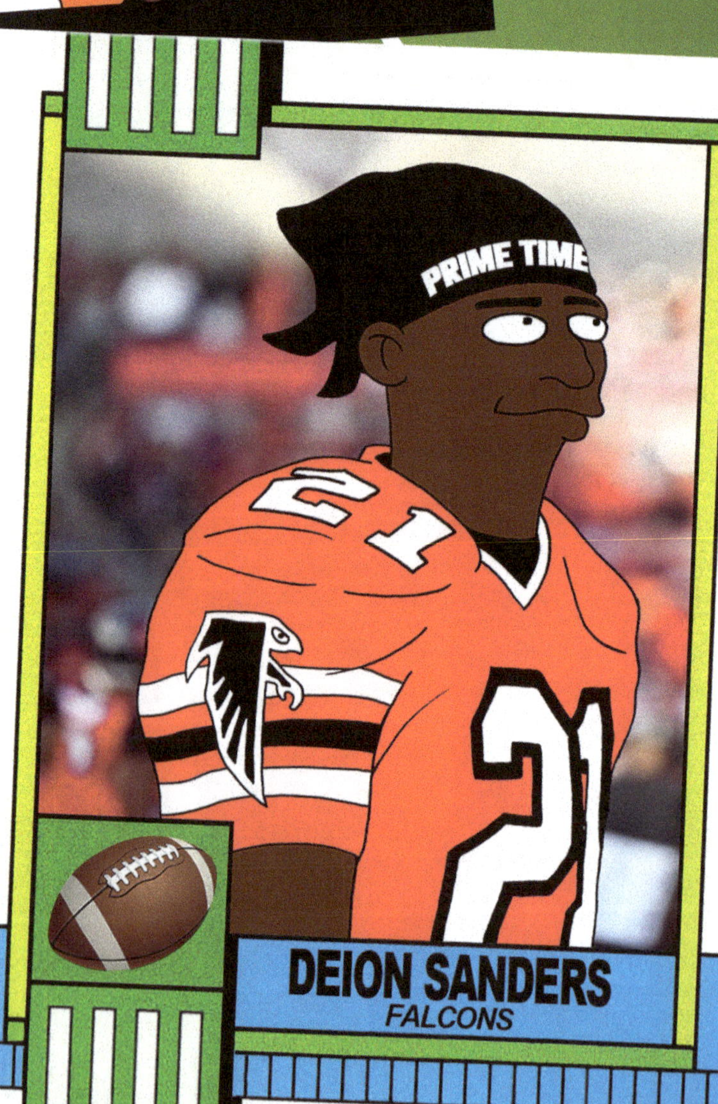

40

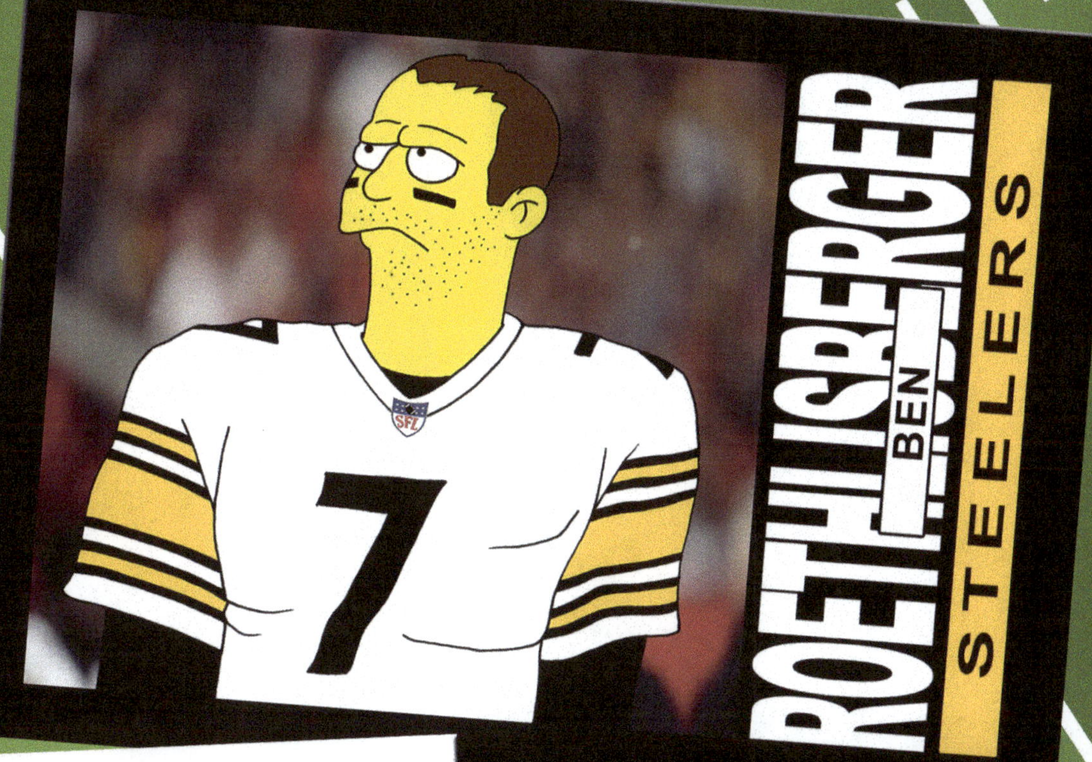
ROETHLISBERGER
BEN
STEELERS
SFL
7

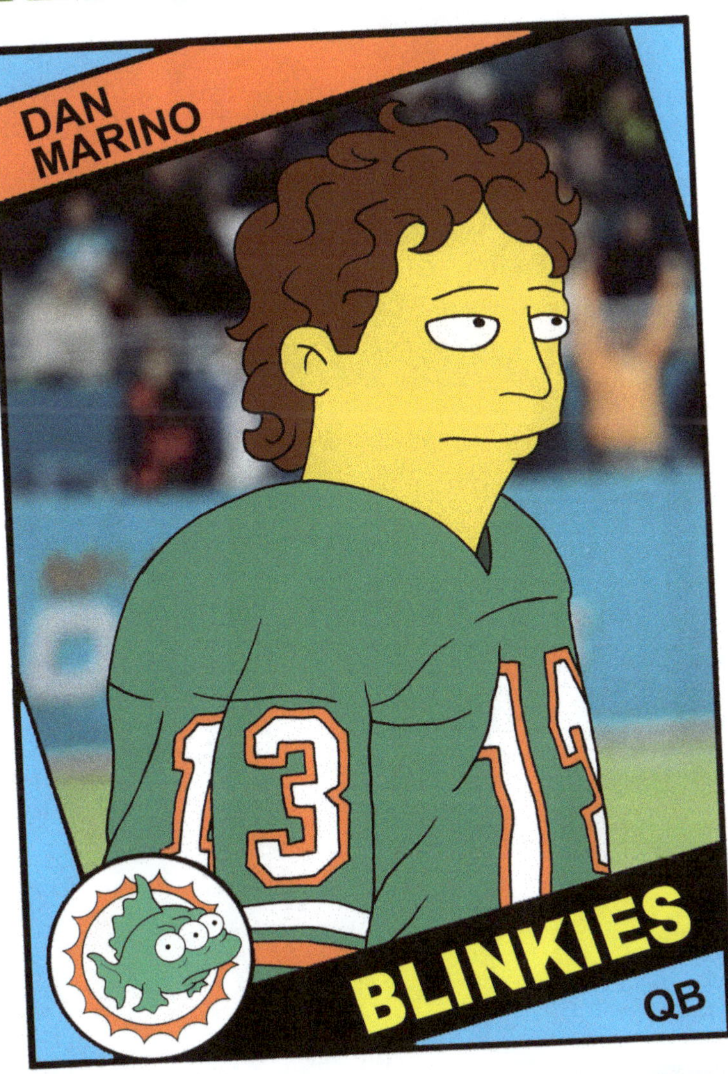
DAN
MARINO
13
BLINKIES
QB

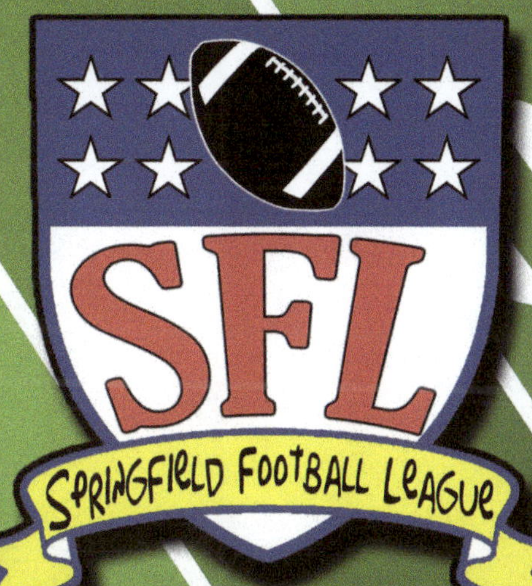
SFL
SPRINGFIELD FOOTBALL LEAGUE

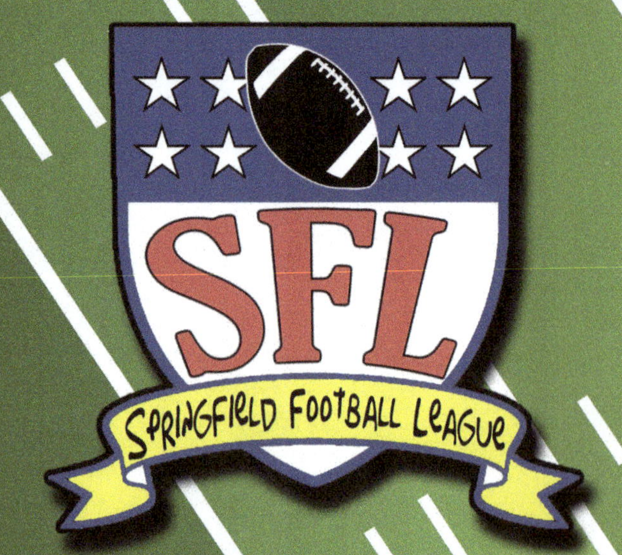
SFL
SPRINGFIELD FOOTBALL LEAGUE

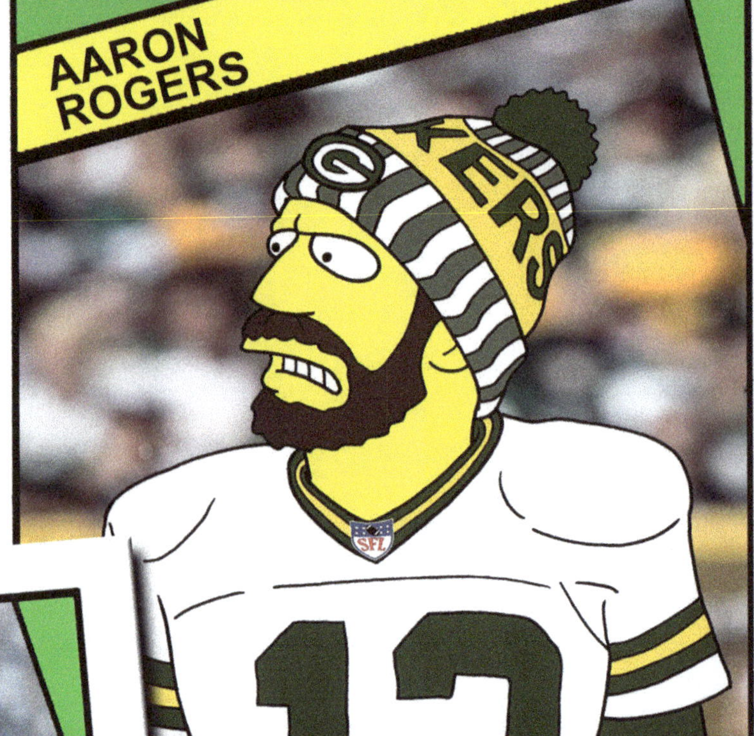
AARON
ROGERS

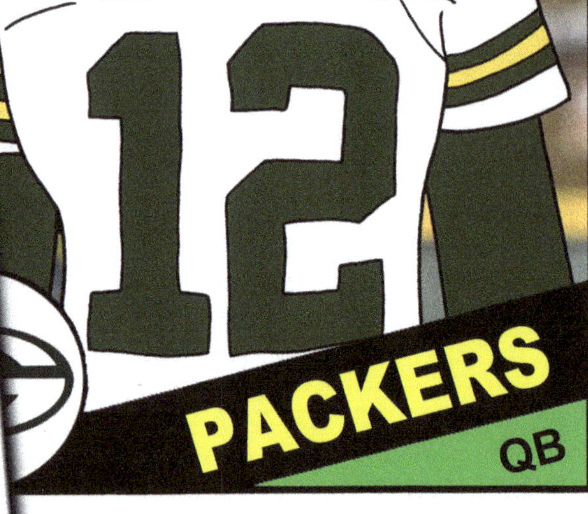
12
PACKERS
QB

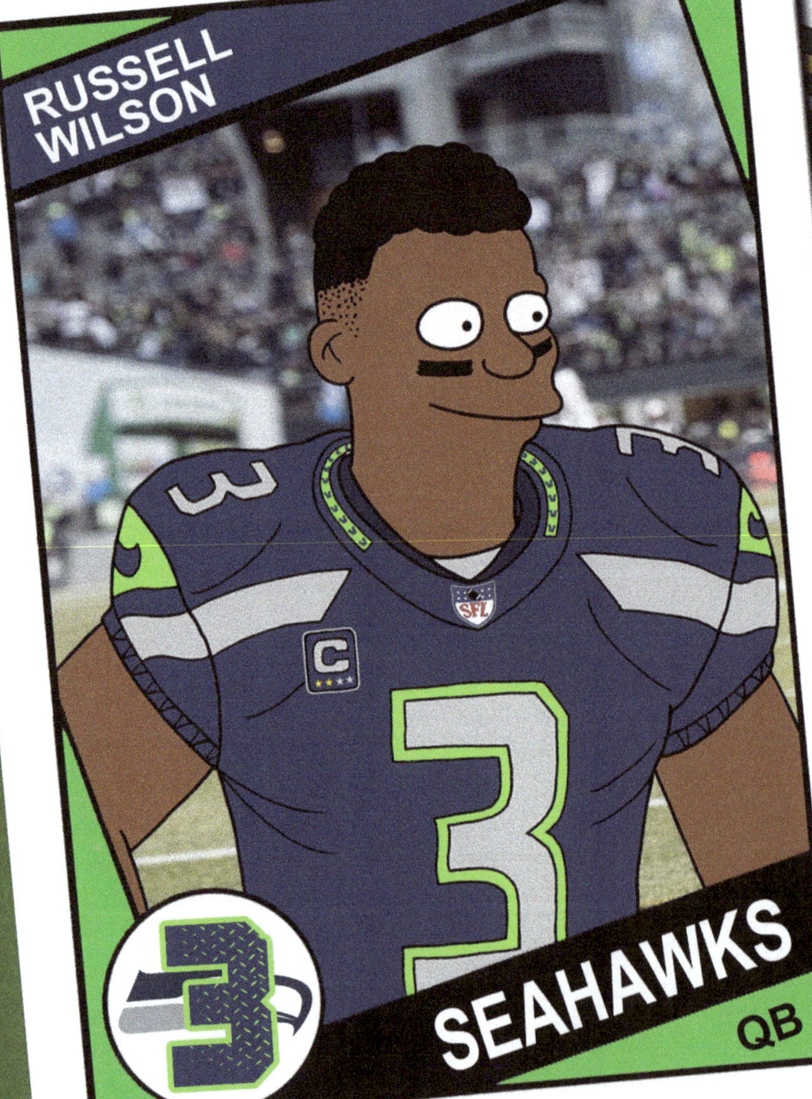
RUSSELL
WILSON
3
SEAHAWKS
QB

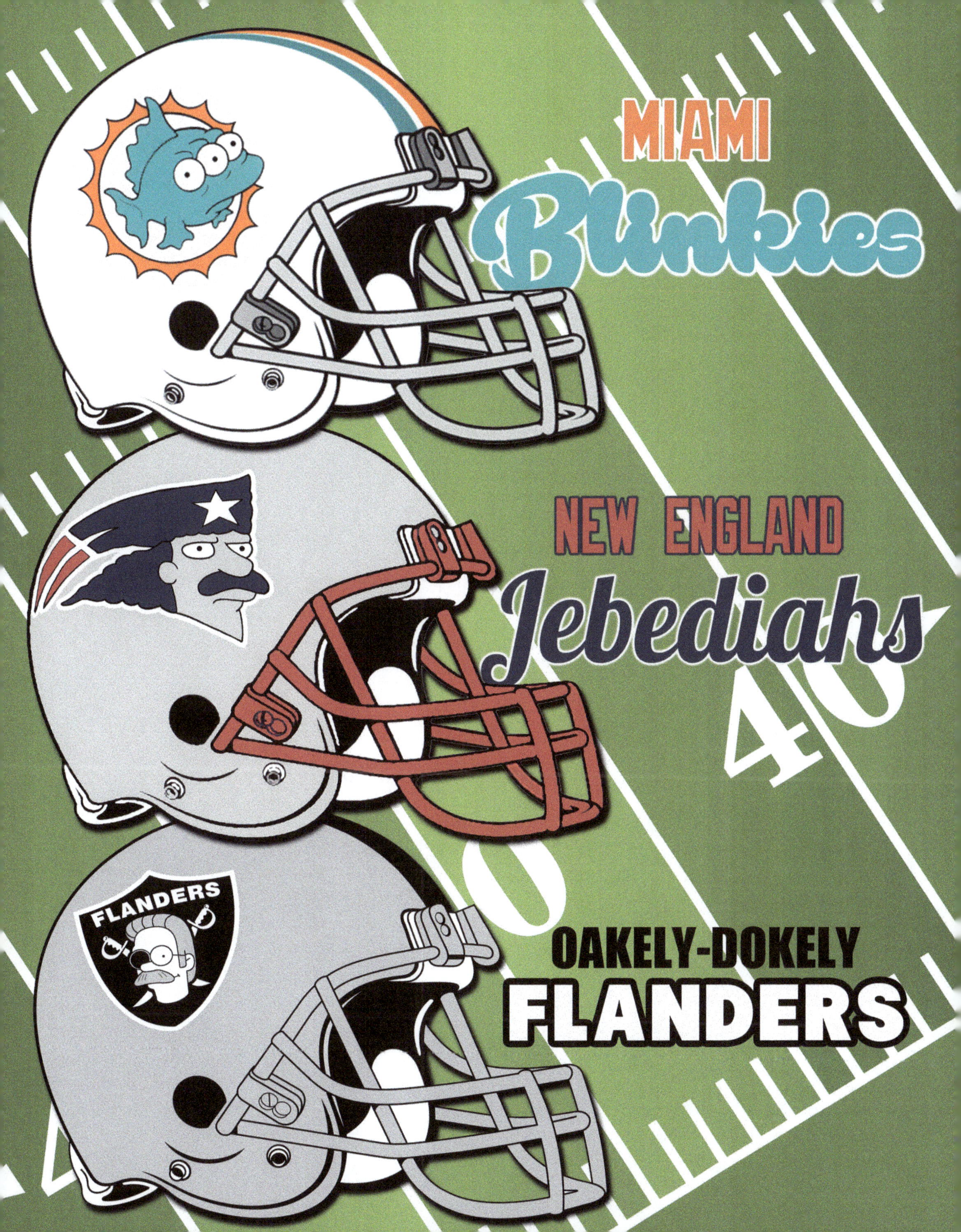
MIAMI
Blinkies
NEW ENGLAND
Jebediahs
40
FLANDERS
OAKELY-DOKELY
FLANDERS

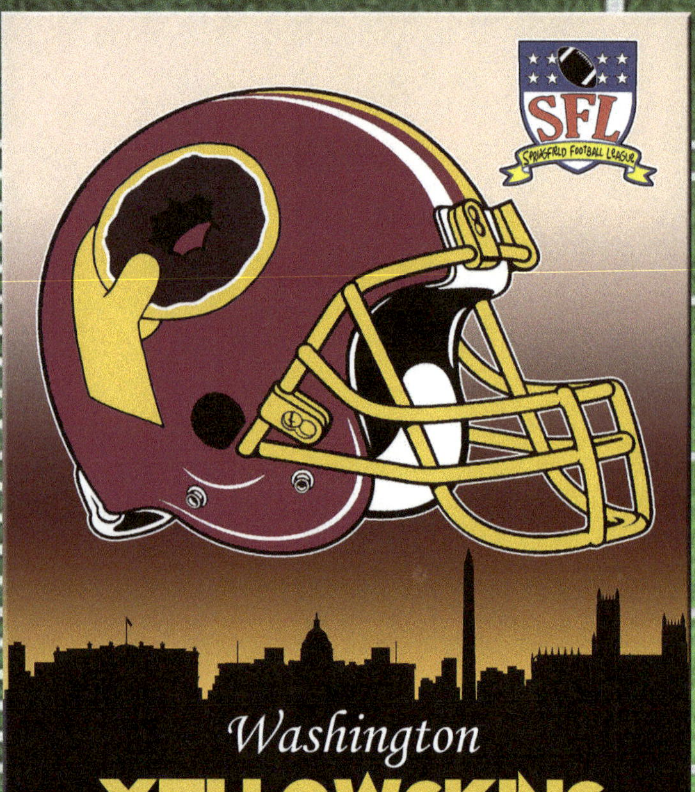

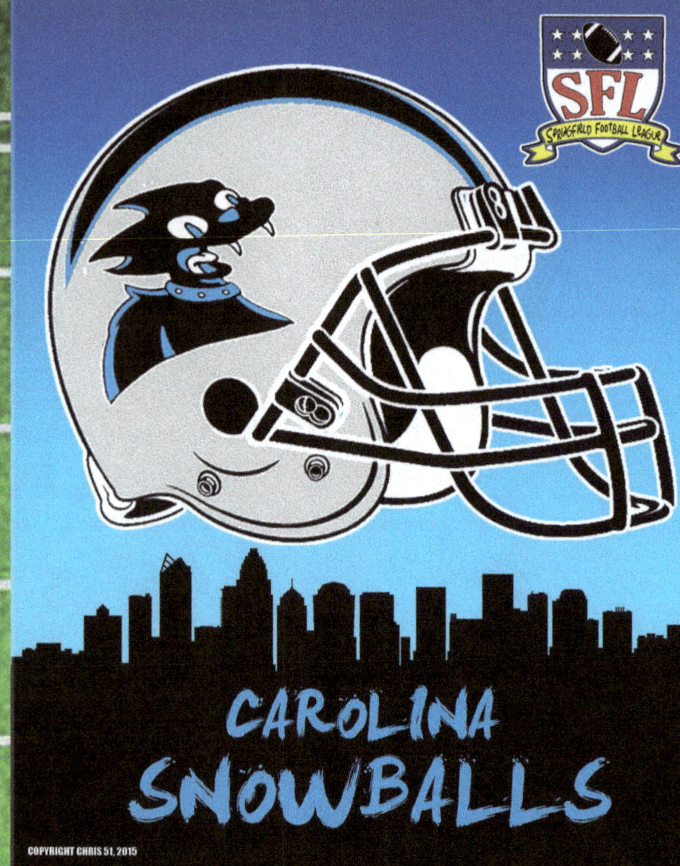

SFL

SPRINGFIELD FOOTBALL LEAGUE

BUFFALO

STAMPYS

COPYRIGHT CHRIS 51, 2015

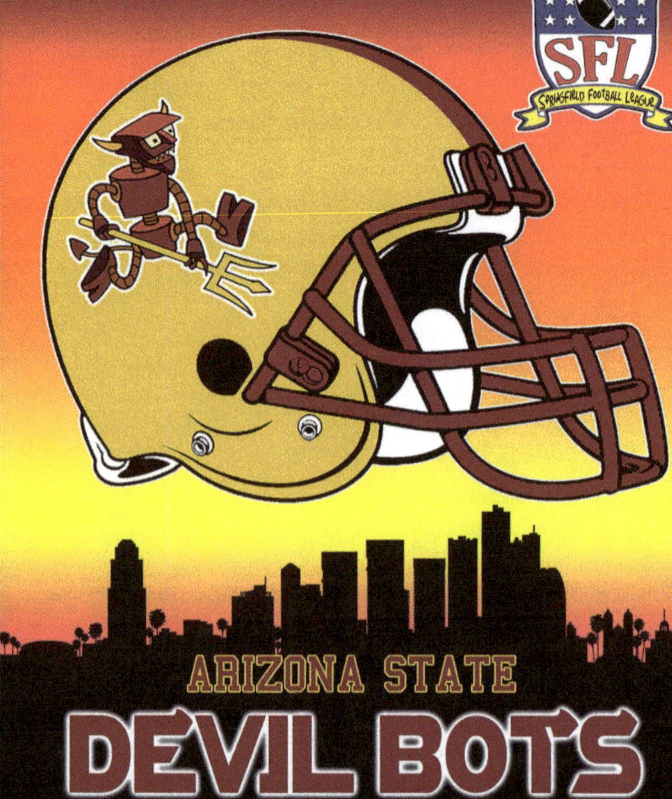

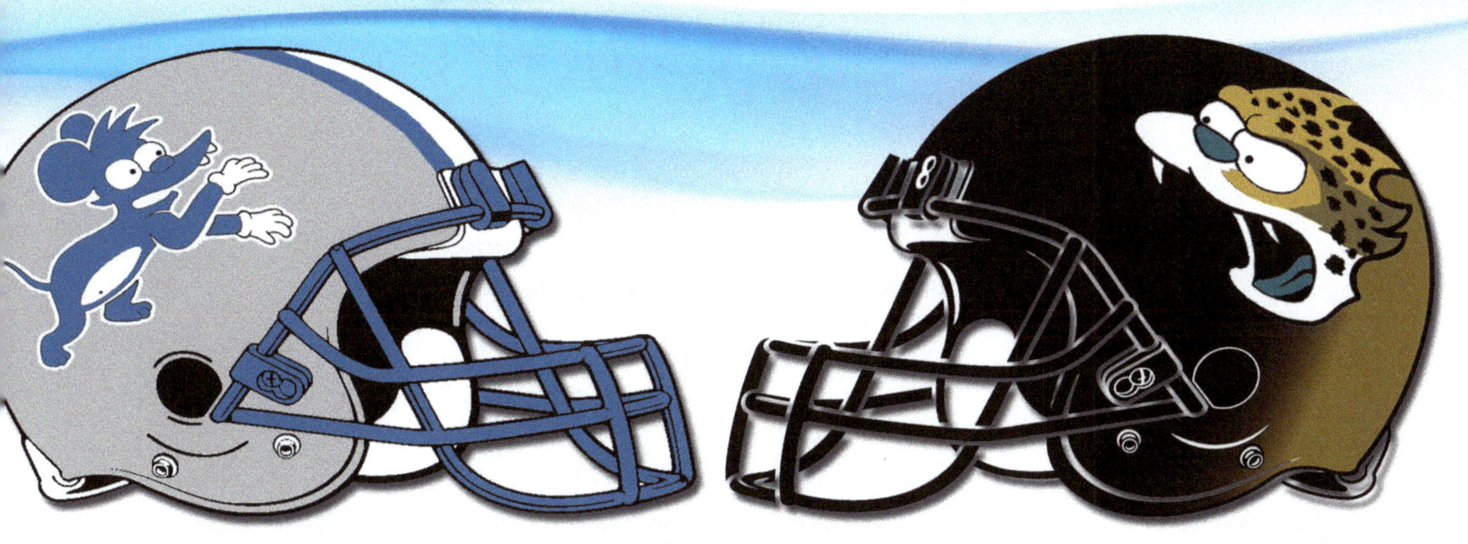

DETROIT
ITCHYS

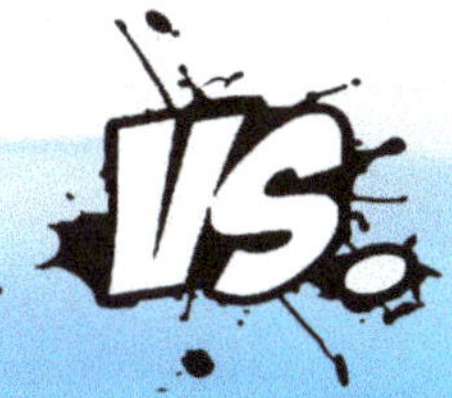

JACKSONVILLE
SCRATCHYS

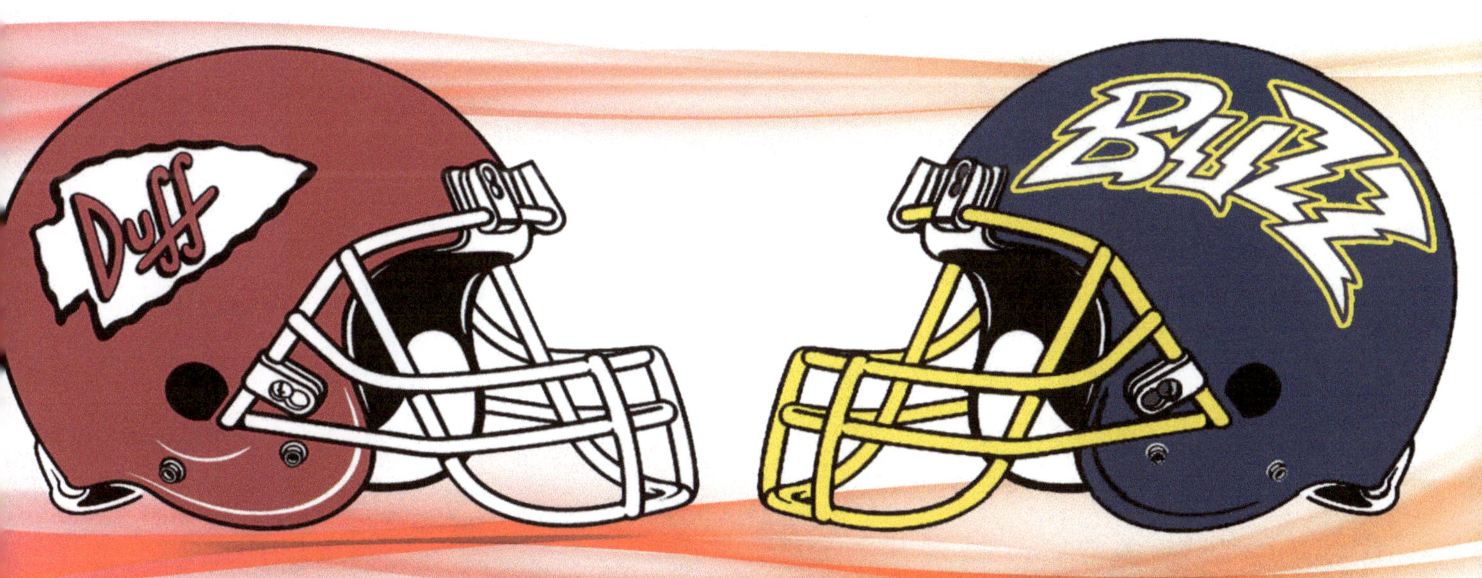

KANSAS CITY
DUFF

SAN DIEGO
BUZZ

JIM AND SILENT SIDESHOW BOB

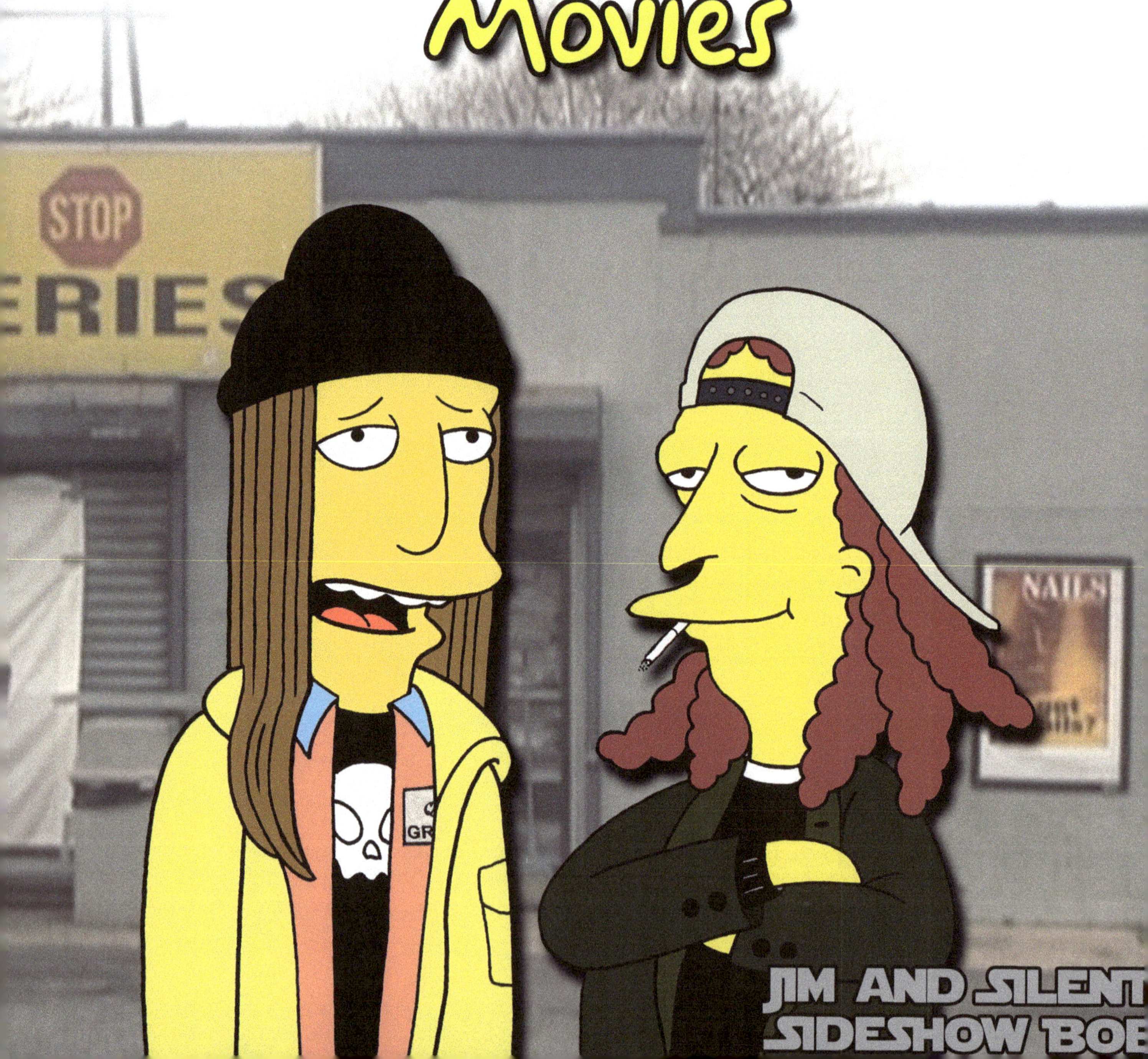

One of my favorite things to do is mashup as much as possible with pop-culture art, characters & themes. Whether it's meshing an established character in a scene that's out of character, or even melding their given names with another character's name, it's always fun.

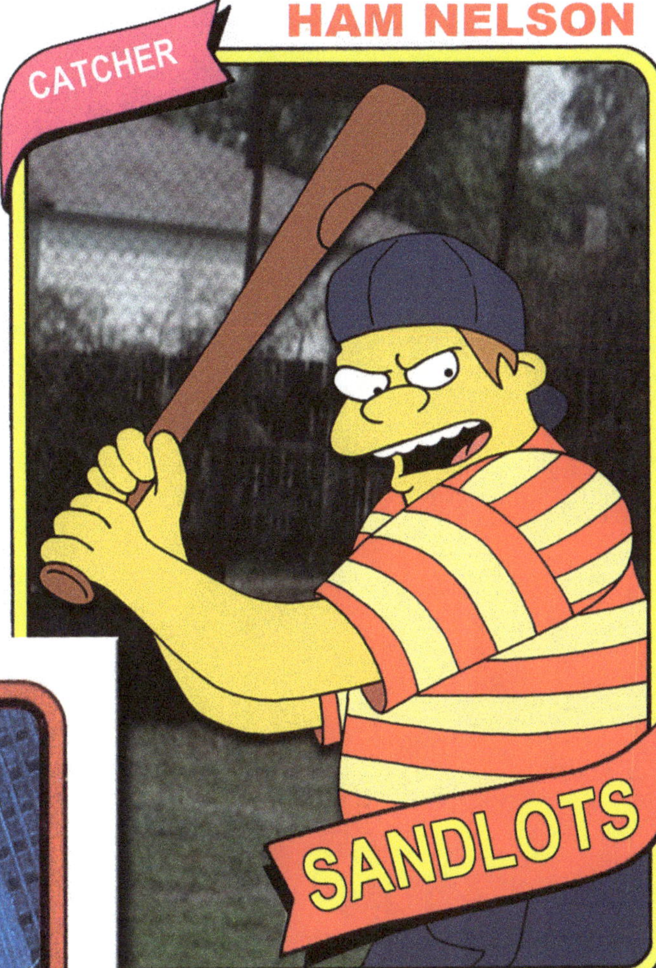

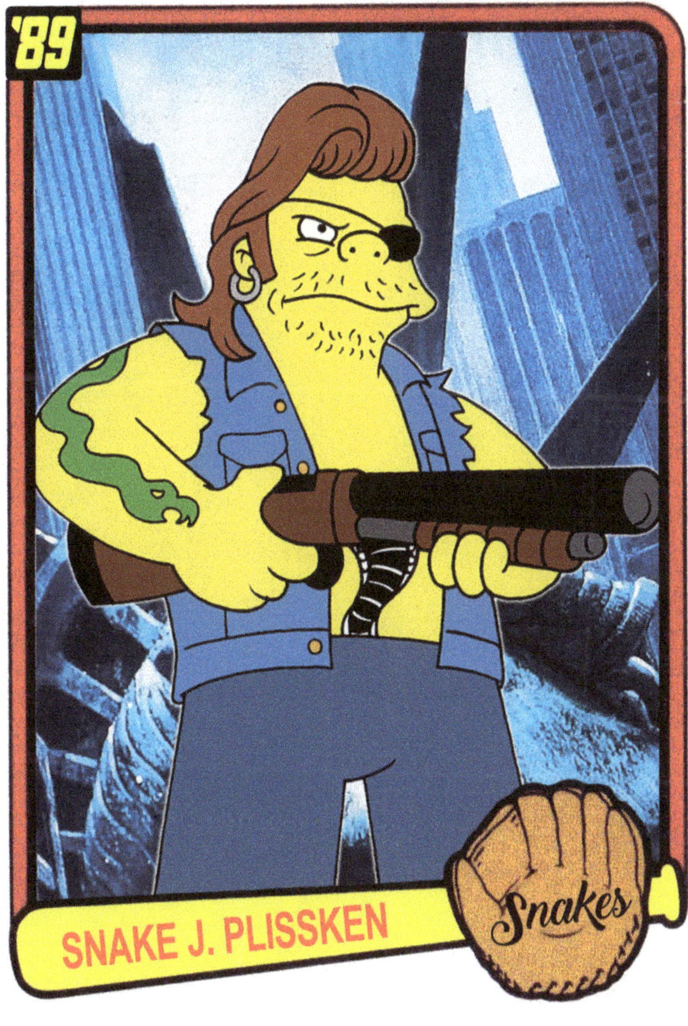

This art is actually a 3-way mashup. I combined old baseball card designs (1) with actual movie footage backgrounds behind "Simpsonized" renditions of movie characters (2) with name combinations from each (3).
Snake Jailbird was the perfect character to combine with the criminal Snake Plissken from Escape from New York (left), and Nelson meets Ham from The Sandlot movie (above).

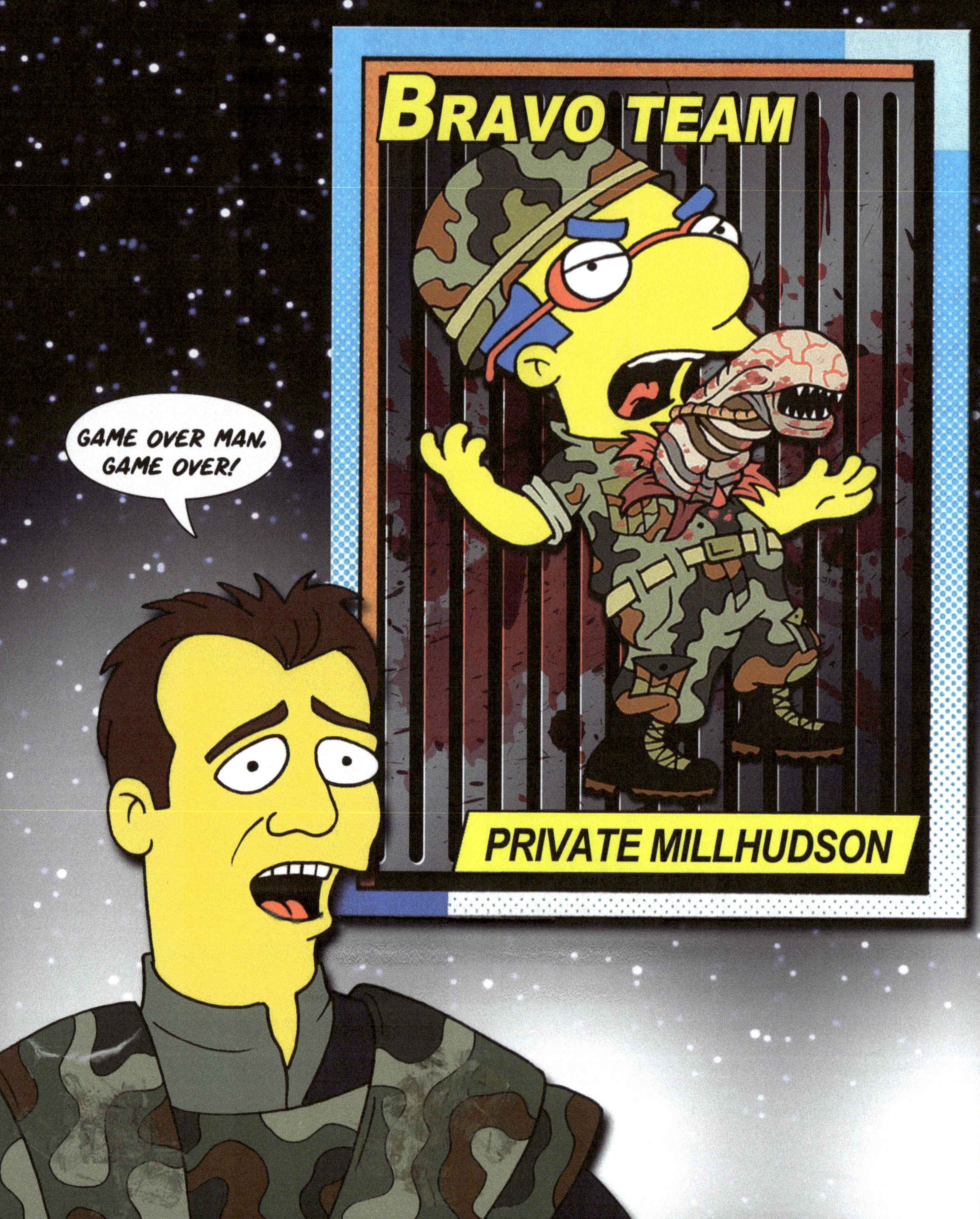
BRAVO TEAM
PRIVATE MILLHUDSON
GAME OVER MAN, GAME OVER!

MOE SZYSLAK

When he pours, he spills.

Cocktail

CHRIS 51 PICTURES
"COCKTAIL"
STARRING
MOE SZYSLAK
HOMER SIMPSON
BARNEY GUMBLE
CARL CARLSON
LENNY LEONARD
CREATED BY
MATT GROENING

R
RESTRICTED

PRINTED IN U.S.A.

NSS # 880056

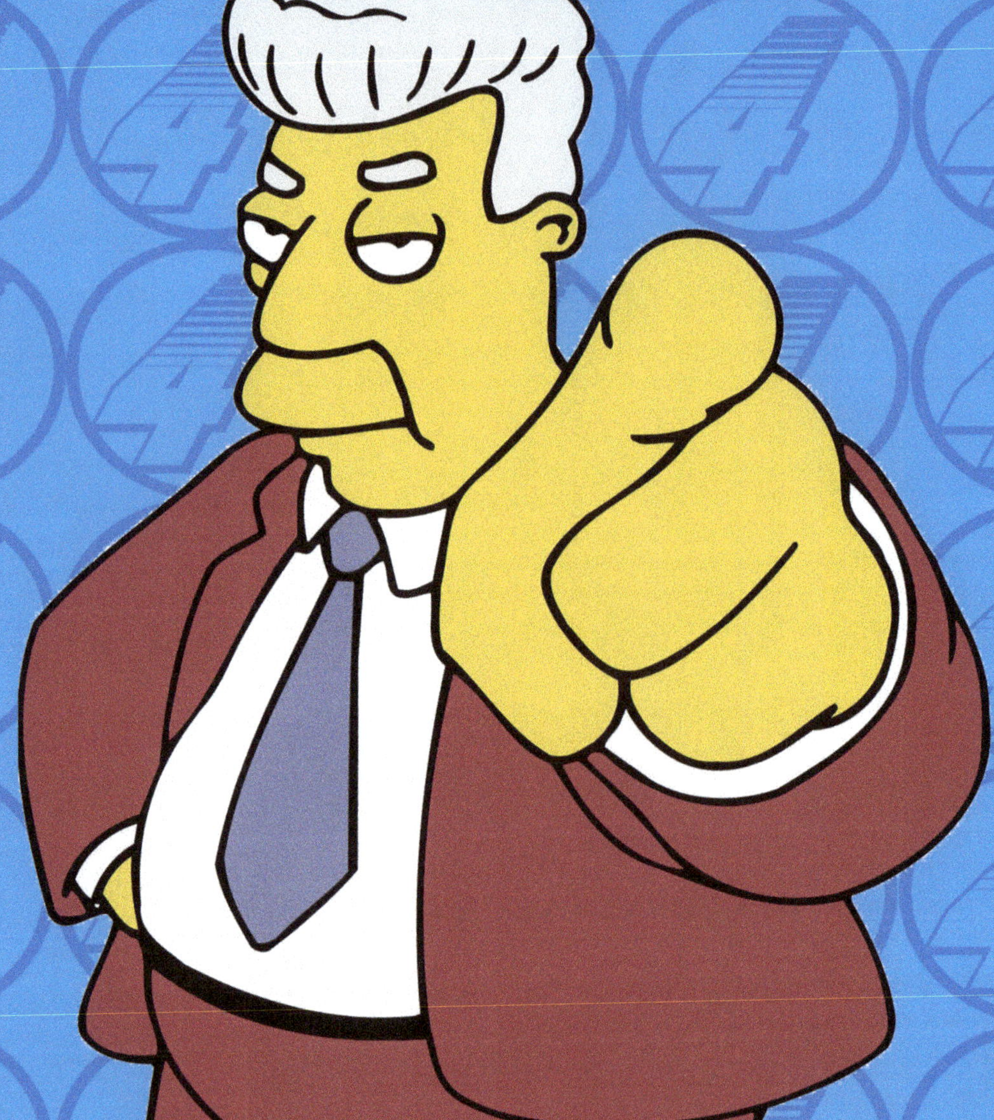
STAY CLASSY SPRINGFIELD
ANCHORMAN
THE LEGEND OF KENT BROCKMAN
A CHRIS 51 PICTURE
STARRING KENT BROCKMAN CREATED BY MATT GROENING
R
RESTRICTED
UNDER 17 REQUIRES ACCOMPANYING PARENT OR ADULT GUARDIAN

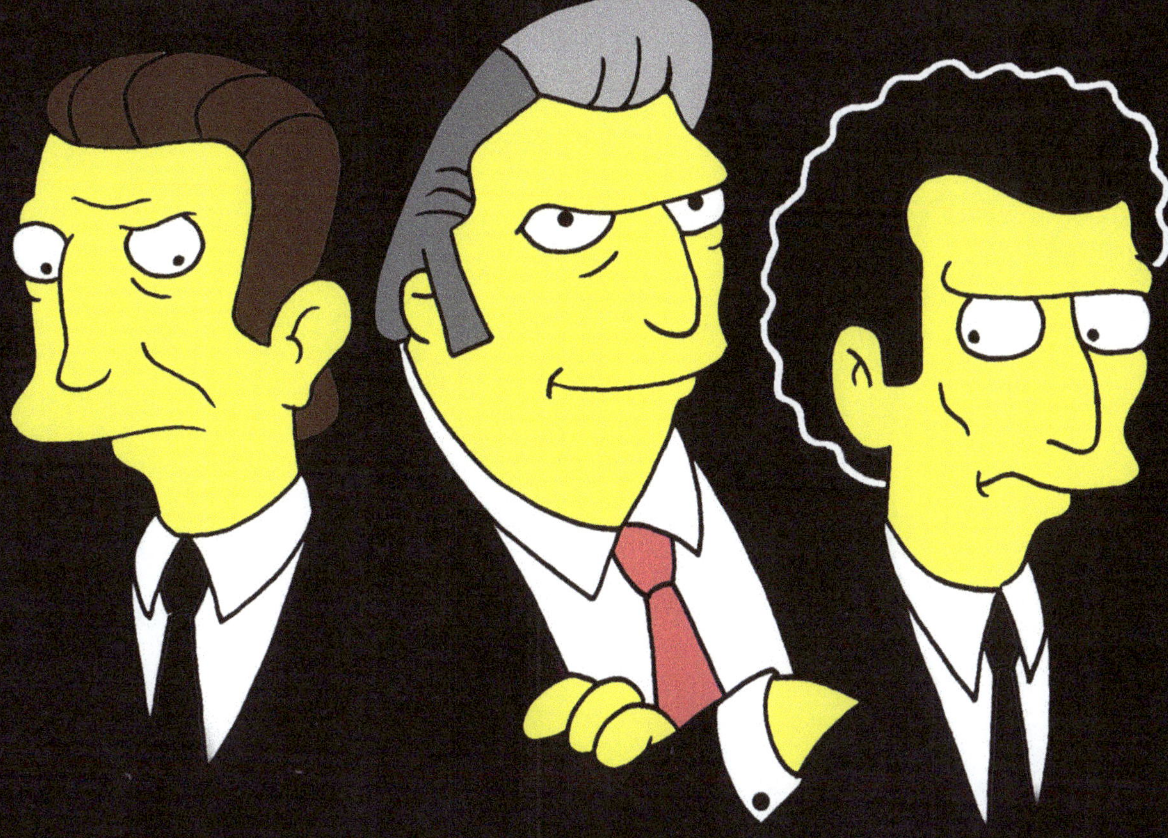
LEGS
FAT TONY
LOUIE
1990 ACADEMY AWARD WINNER
BEST SUPPORTING GANGSTER - LOUIE
FatFellas
--A CHRIS 51 PICTURE--
Three Decades of Mafia in Springfield
DVD
VIDEO

Twelve donuts. One cop.
The calories are against The Chief...
That's just the way he likes it.

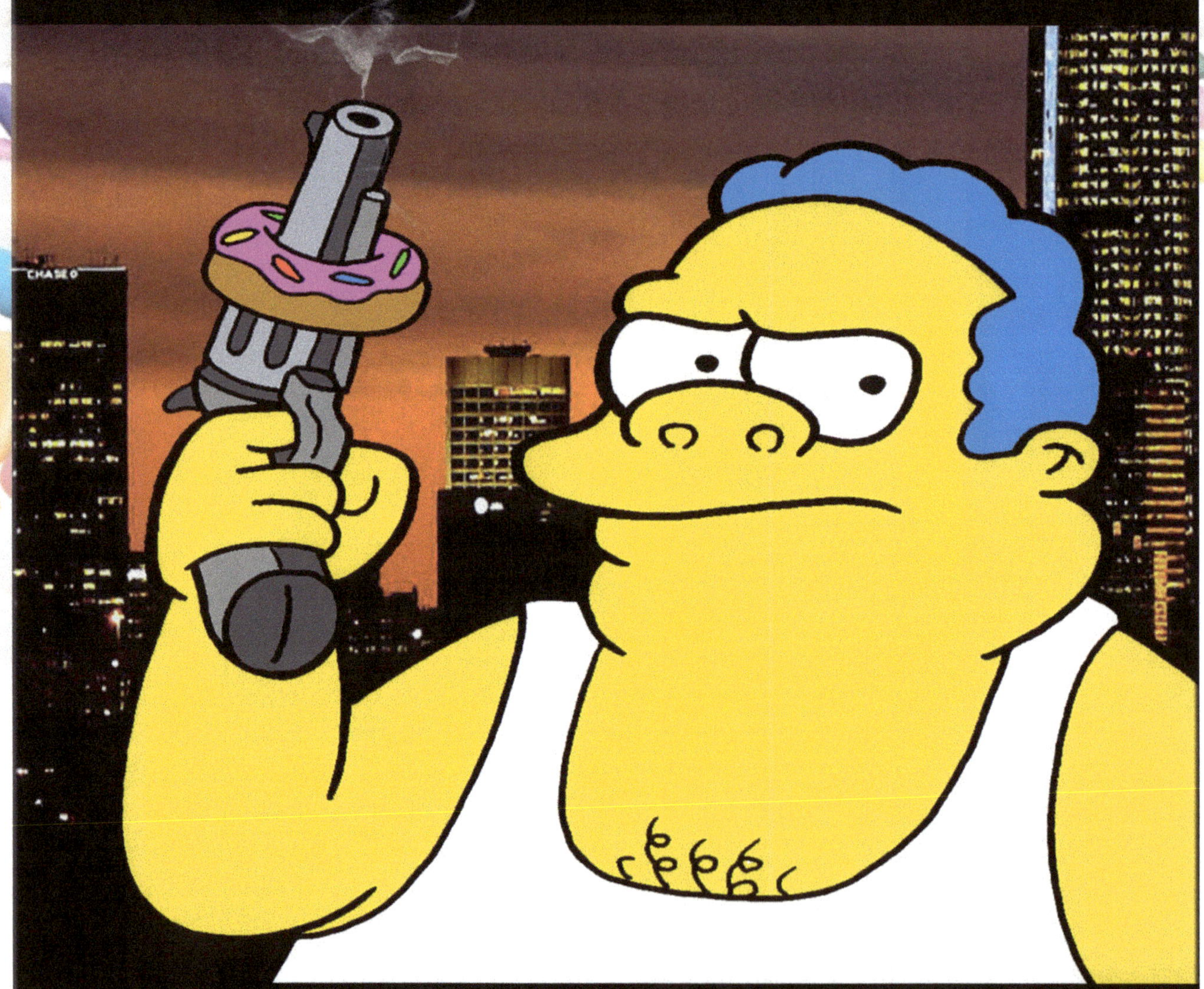

CLANCY WIGGUM

DIET HARD

CHRIS 51 Presents AN ALPHA GEEK PRODUCTION
Starring CLANCY WIGGUM SERGEANT LOU OFFICER EDDIE SNAKE
COMING TO A BAKERY NEAR YOU

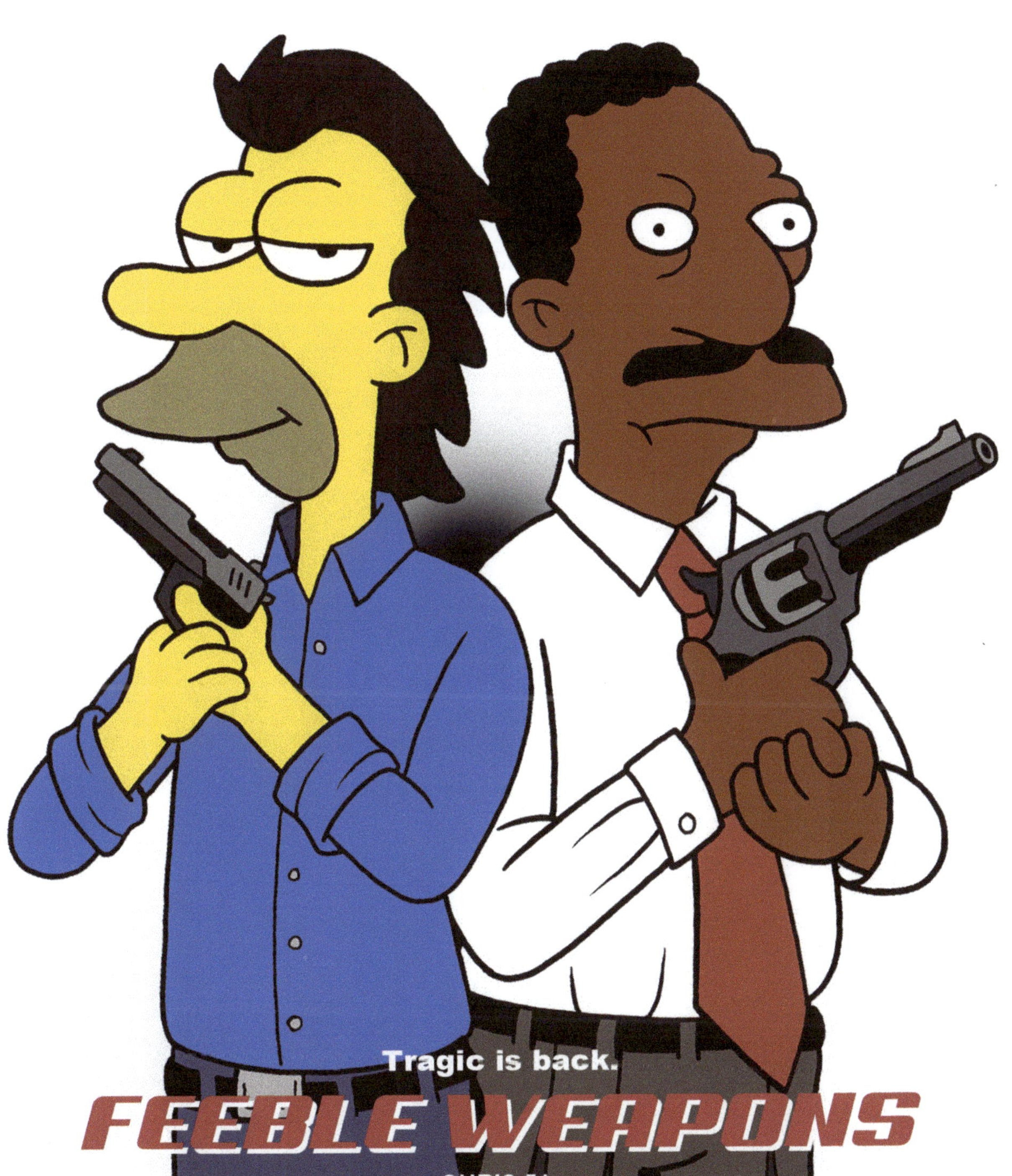
LENNY LEONARD
CARL CARLSON
Tragic is back.
FEEBLE WEAPONS
A CHRIS 51 Film

IN LOVING MEMORY

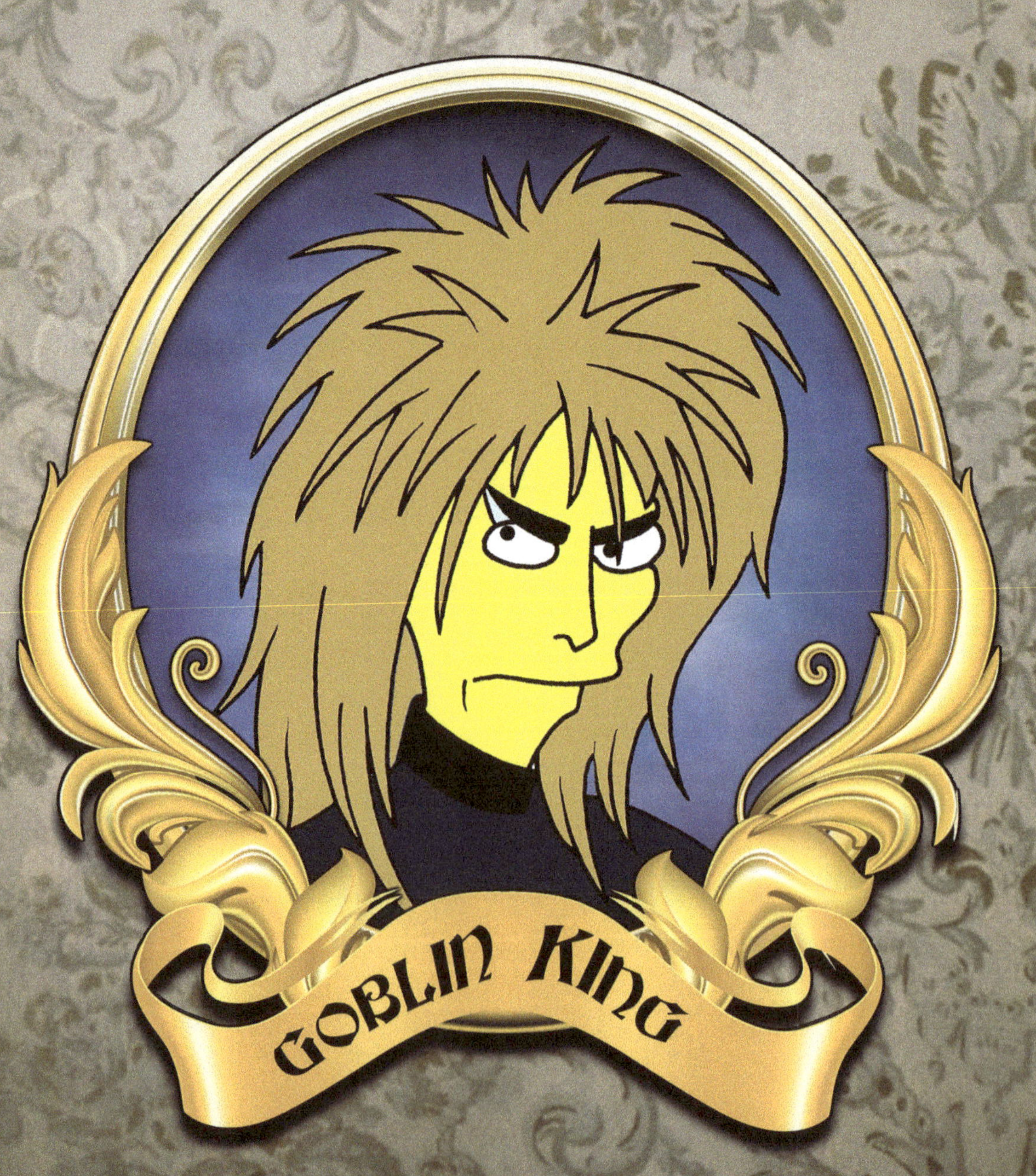

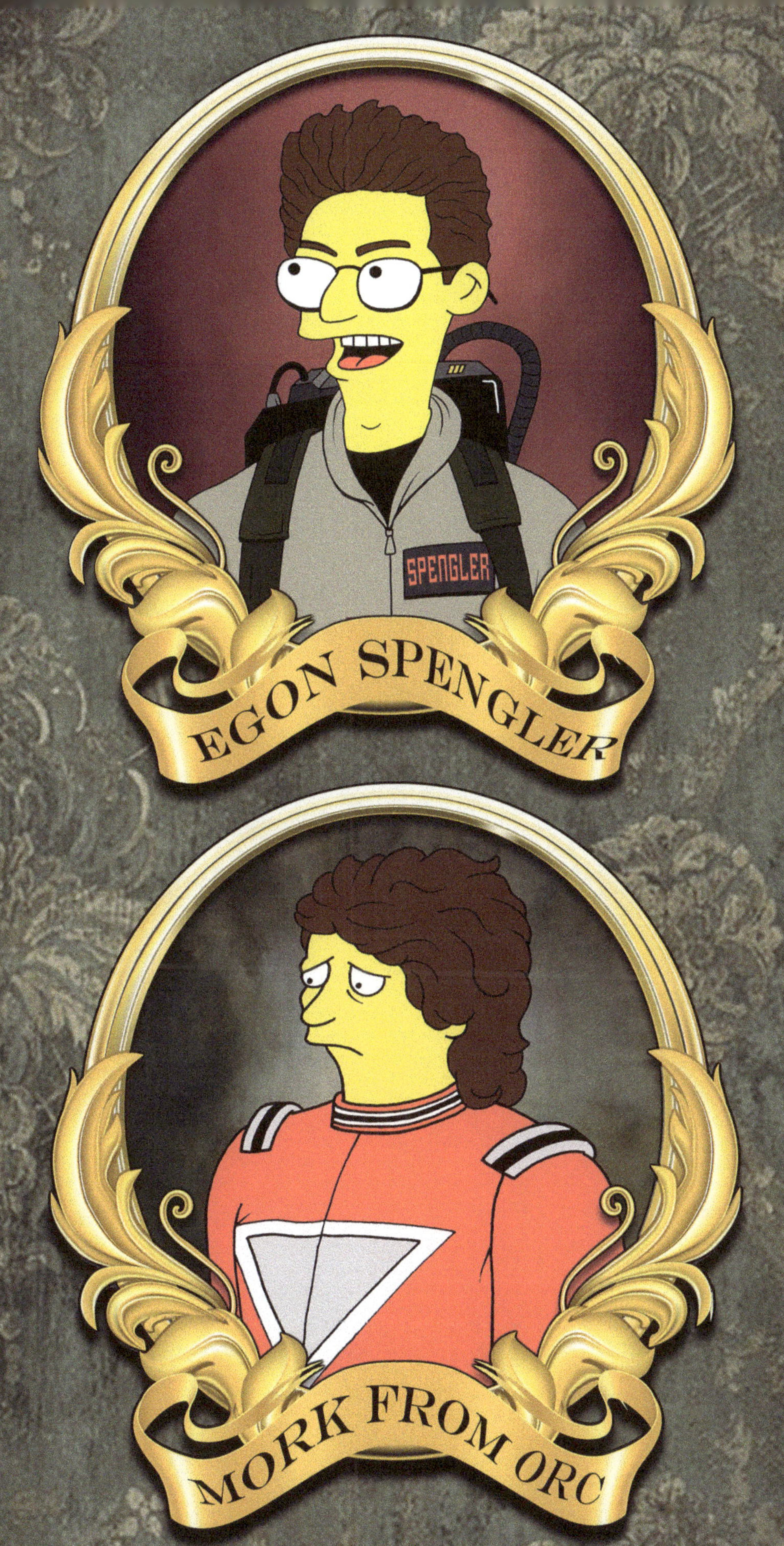
SPENGLER
EGON SPENGLER
MORK FROM ORC

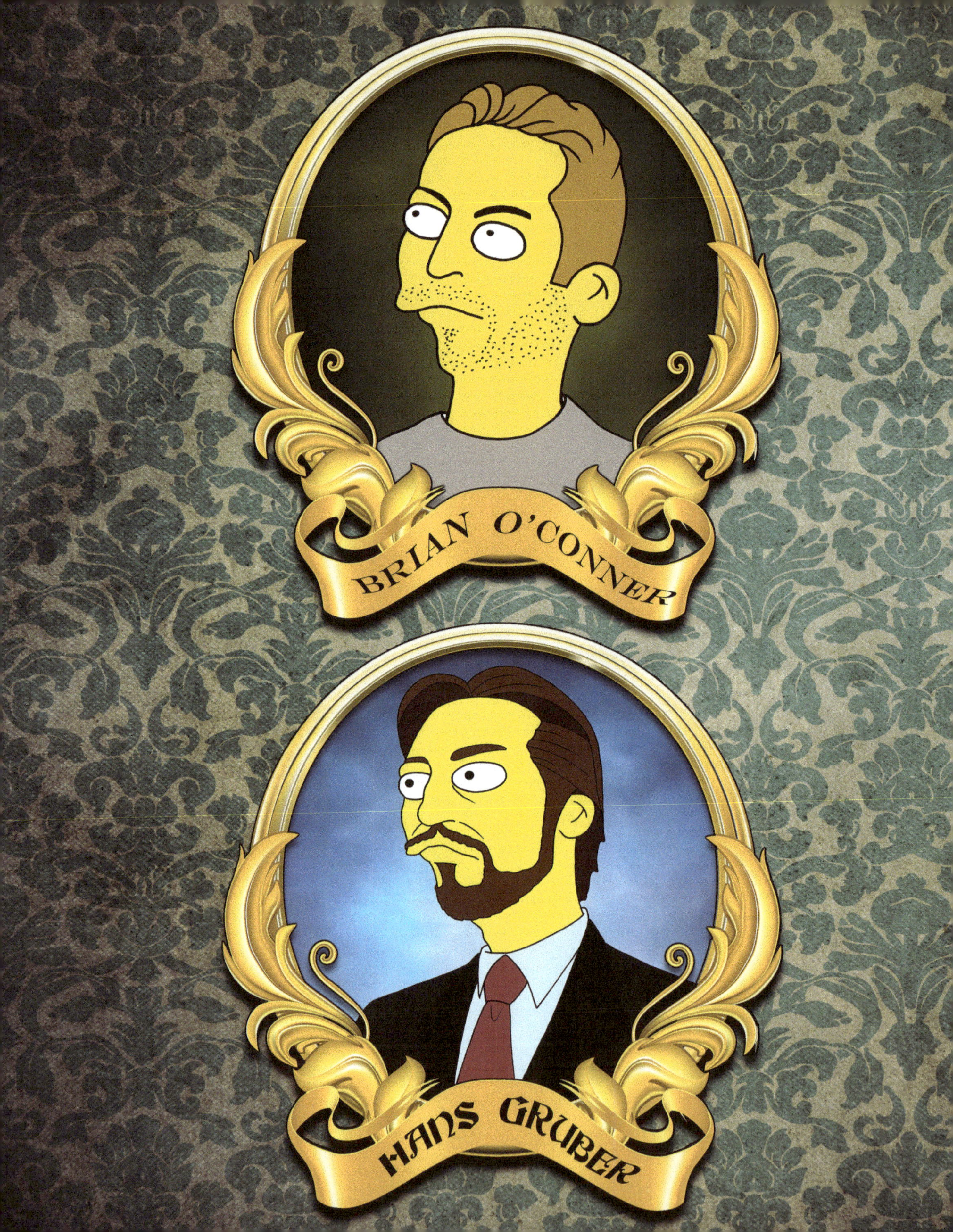
BRIAN O'CONNER
HANS GRUBER

Chapter 7

Comics

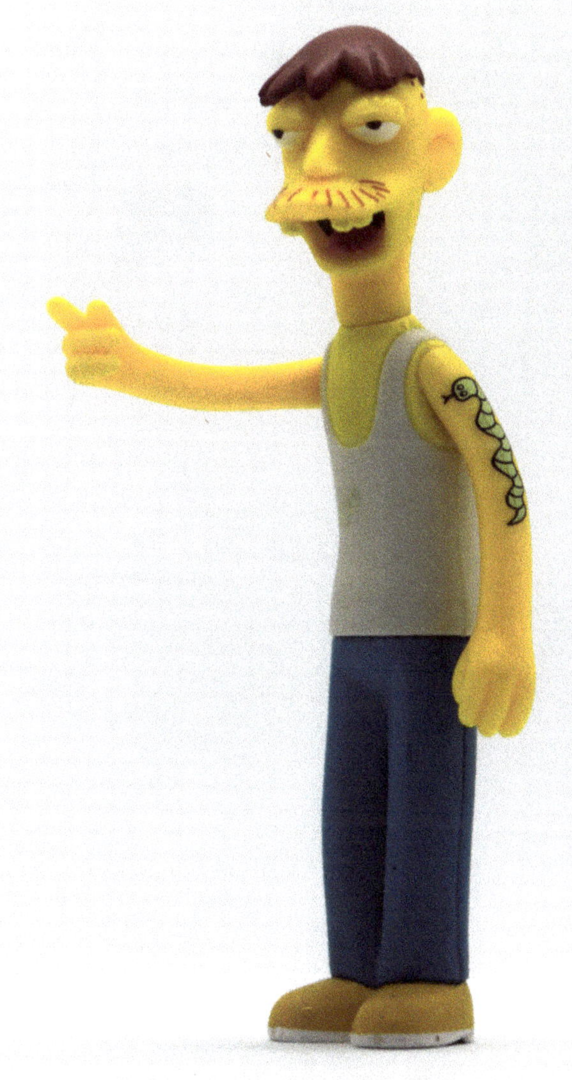

In my first official involvement in a comic, I created the art) for these panels.

Editor James Harvey asked legendary comic artist Mike Allred to contribute to his new Bartkira project. Mike suggested to James that I do it with him, knowing what a huge Simpsons fan I was. It was a dream opportunity that I tackled with all my heart. I could have never done it without the Allreds. They did the colors and background; which made it even more meaningful as a collaboration with two legends in the comic industry!

James wanted Bart and Laura Powers to see Milhouse and Nelson as ghosts riding by them, as an adaptation of the Akira characters in a current panel.

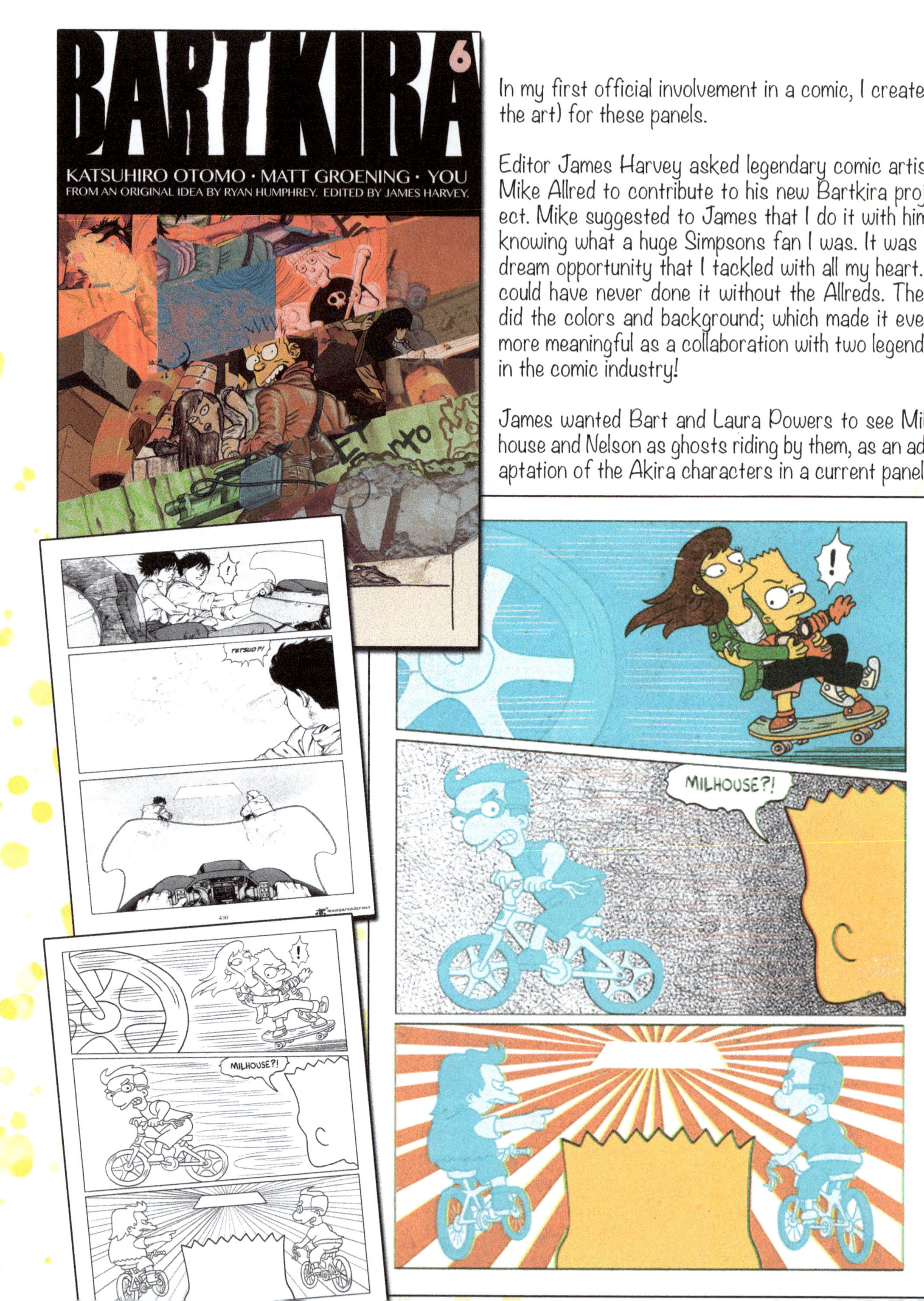

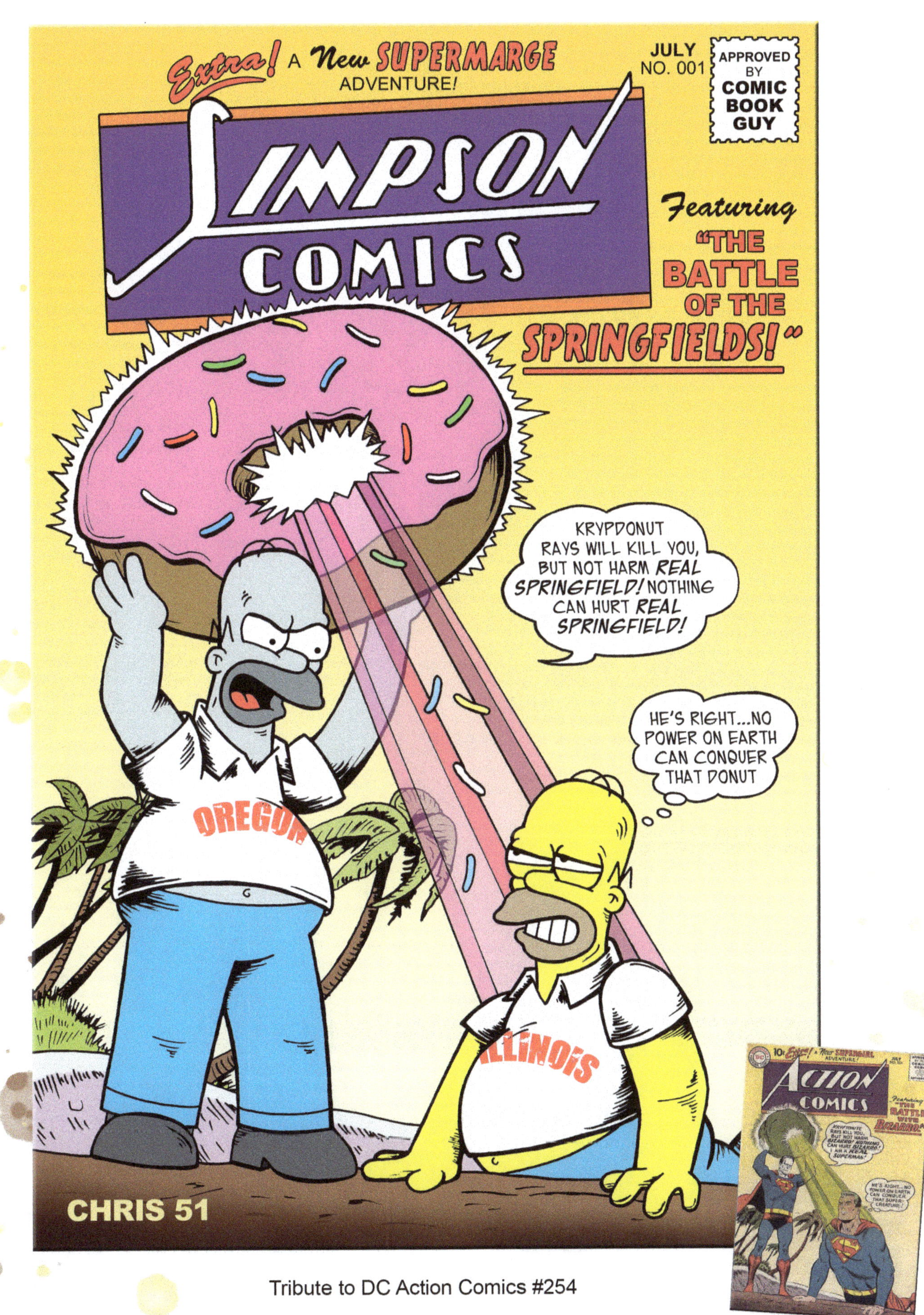

Tribute to DC Action Comics #254

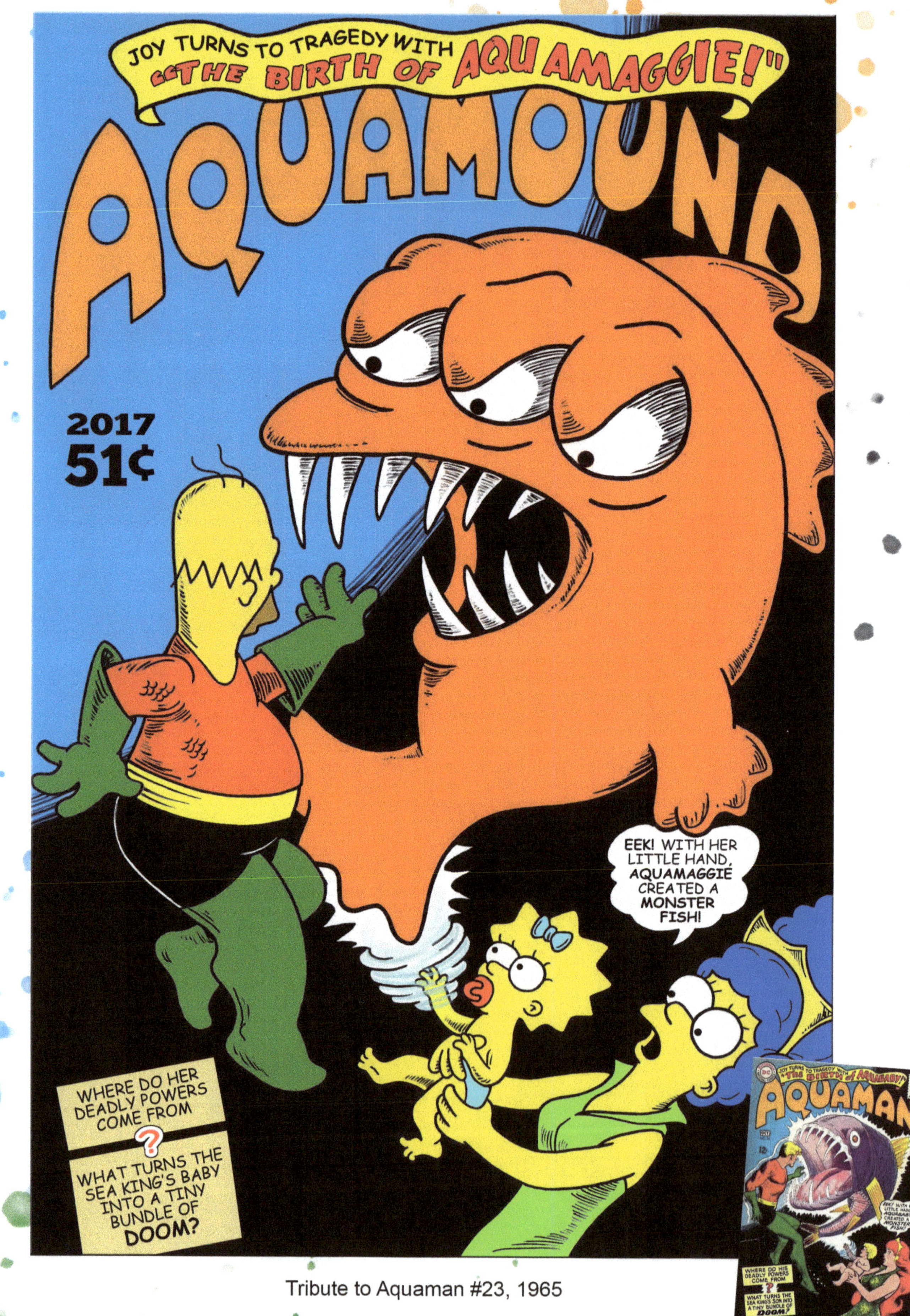

Tribute to Aquaman #23, 1965

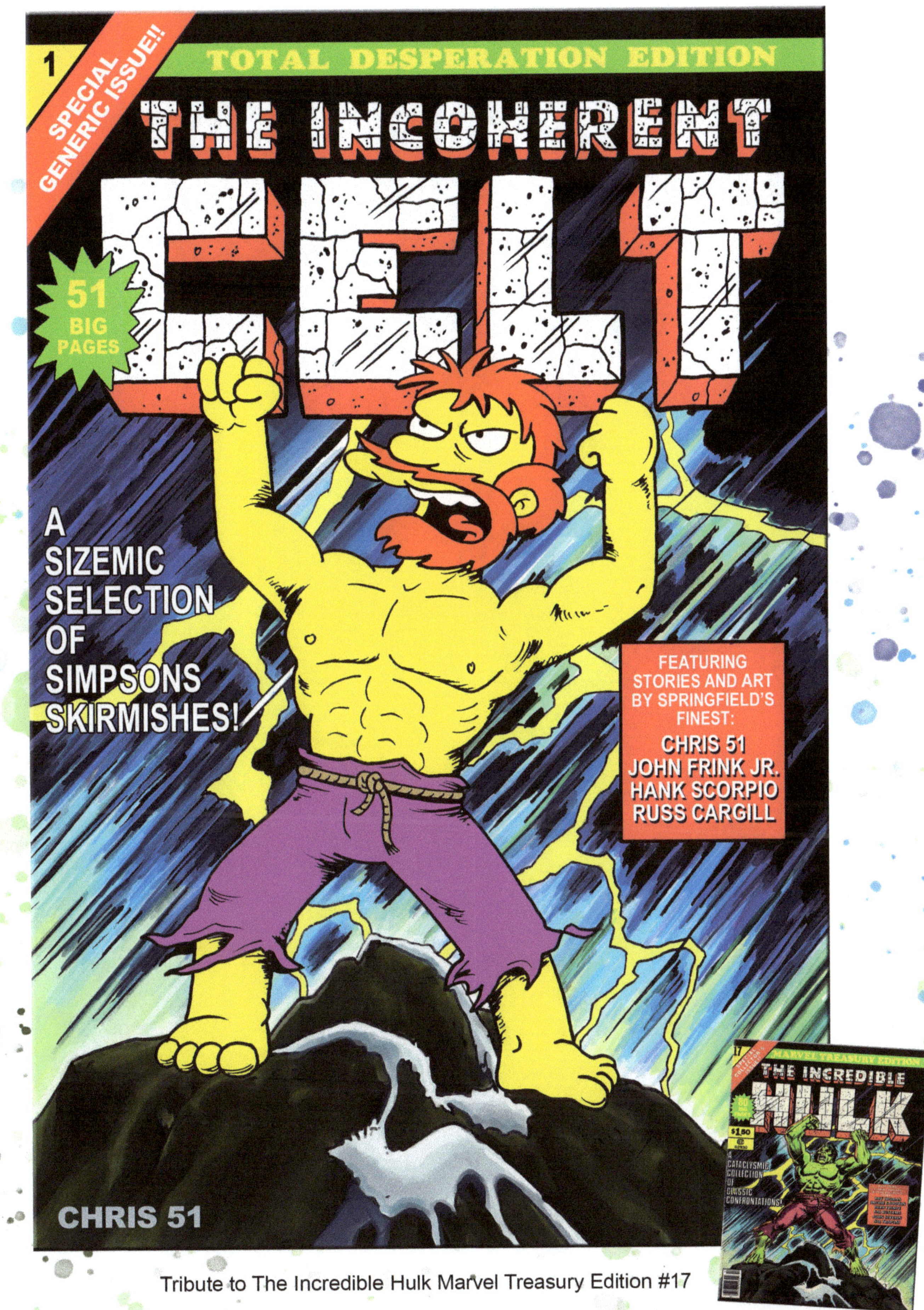

Tribute to The Incredible Hulk Marvel Treasury Edition #17

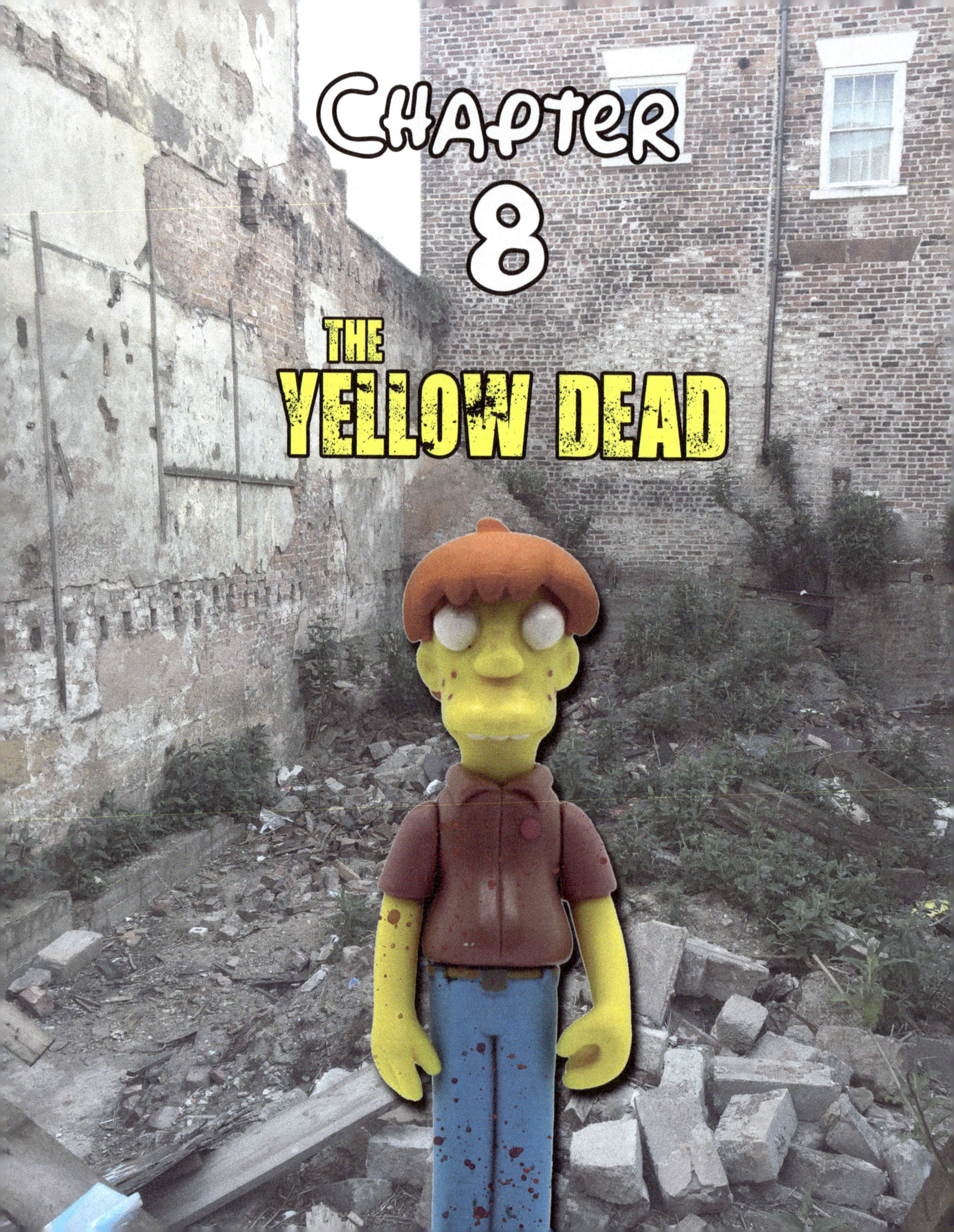
Chapter
8
THE
YELLOW DEAD

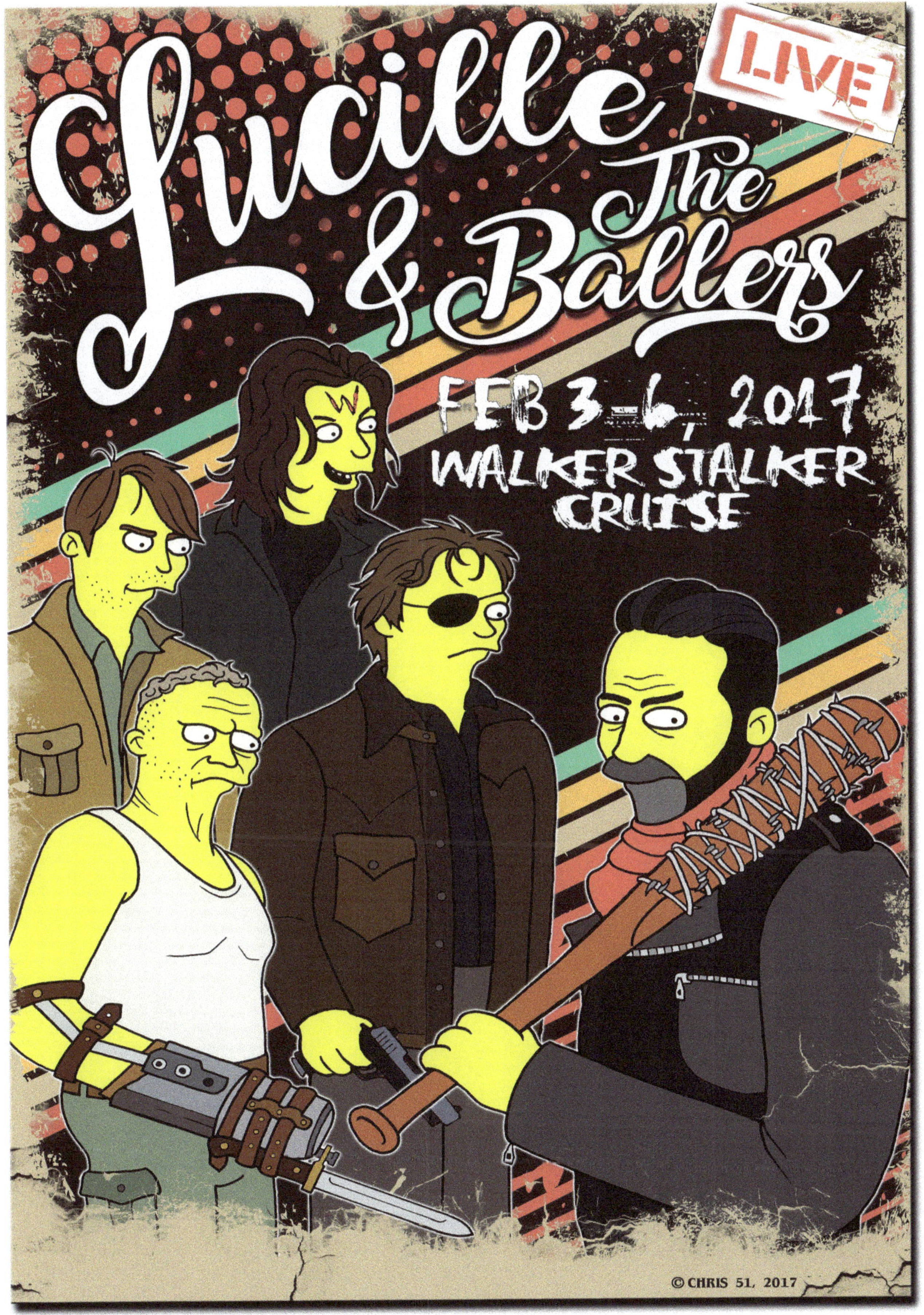

Limited Edition print made for Walker Stalker Cruise 2017

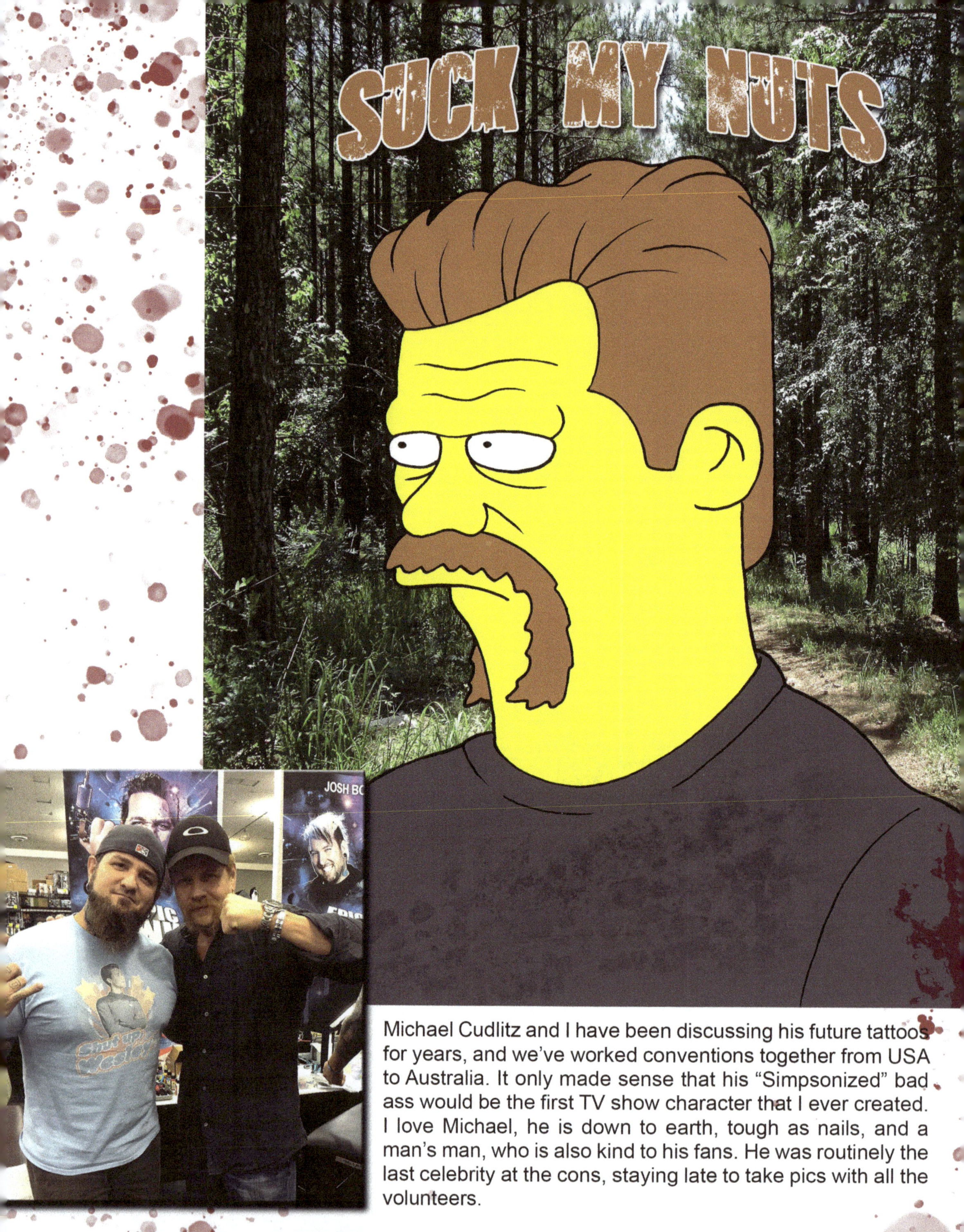

Michael Cudlitz and I have been discussing his future tattoos for years, and we've worked conventions together from USA to Australia. It only made sense that his "Simpsonized" bad ass would be the first TV show character that I ever created. I love Michael, he is down to earth, tough as nails, and a man's man, who is also kind to his fans. He was routinely the last celebrity at the cons, staying late to take pics with all the volunteers.

DR. SMARTY PANTS

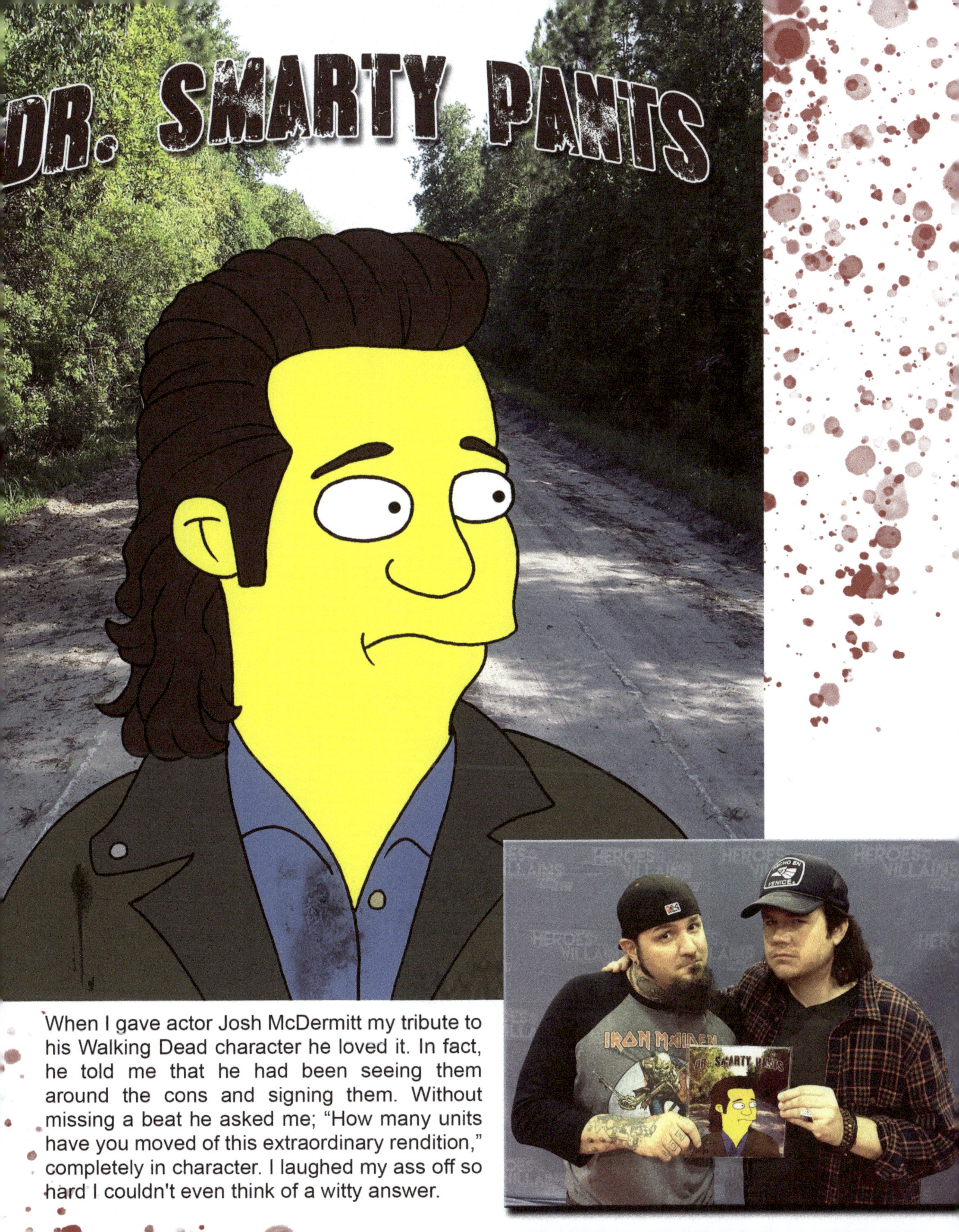

When I gave actor Josh McDermitt my tribute to his Walking Dead character he loved it. In fact, he told me that he had been seeing them around the cons and signing them. Without missing a beat he asked me; "How many units have you moved of this extraordinary rendition," completely in character. I laughed my ass off so hard I couldn't even think of a witty answer.

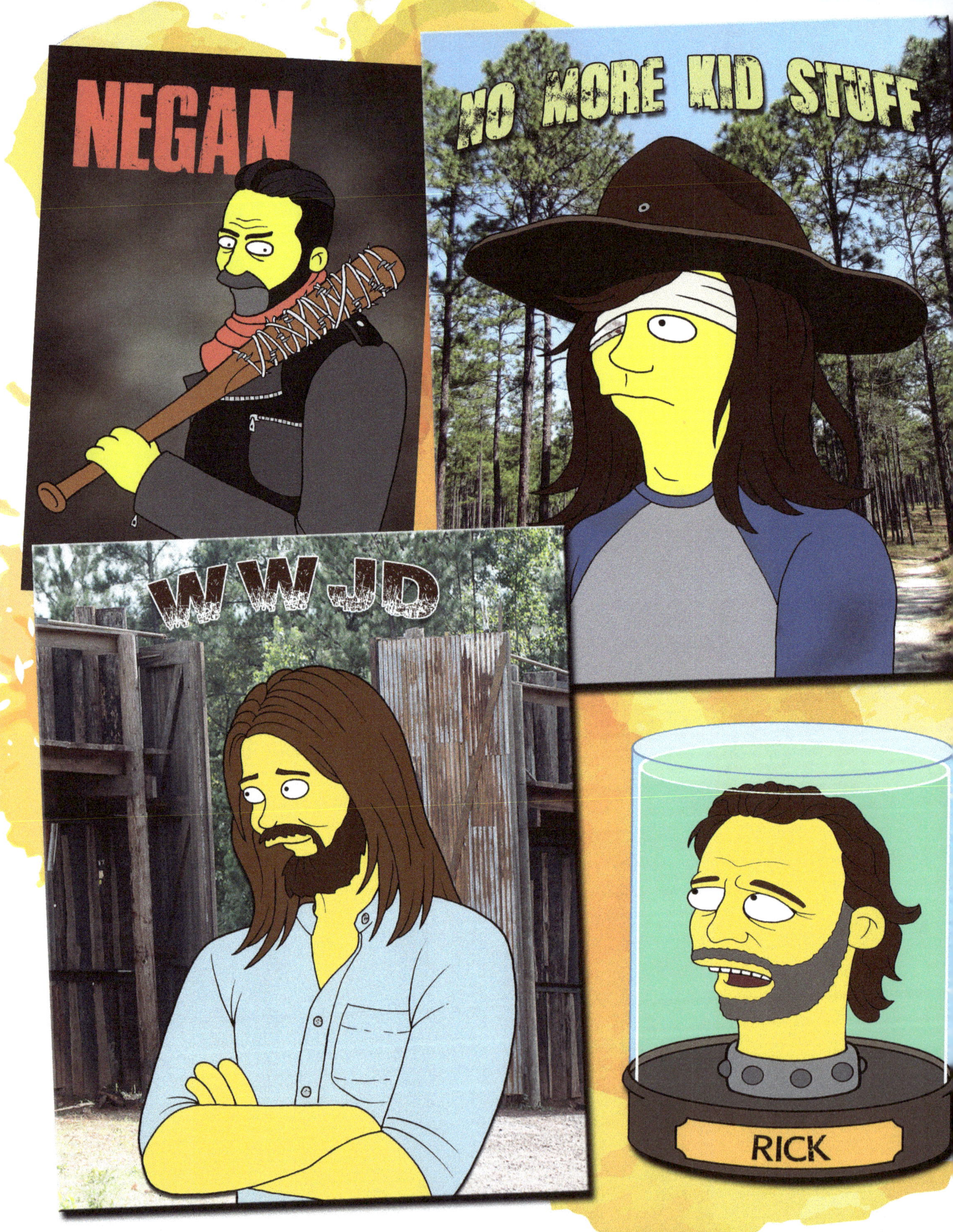
NEGAN
NO MORE KID STUFF
WWJD
RICK

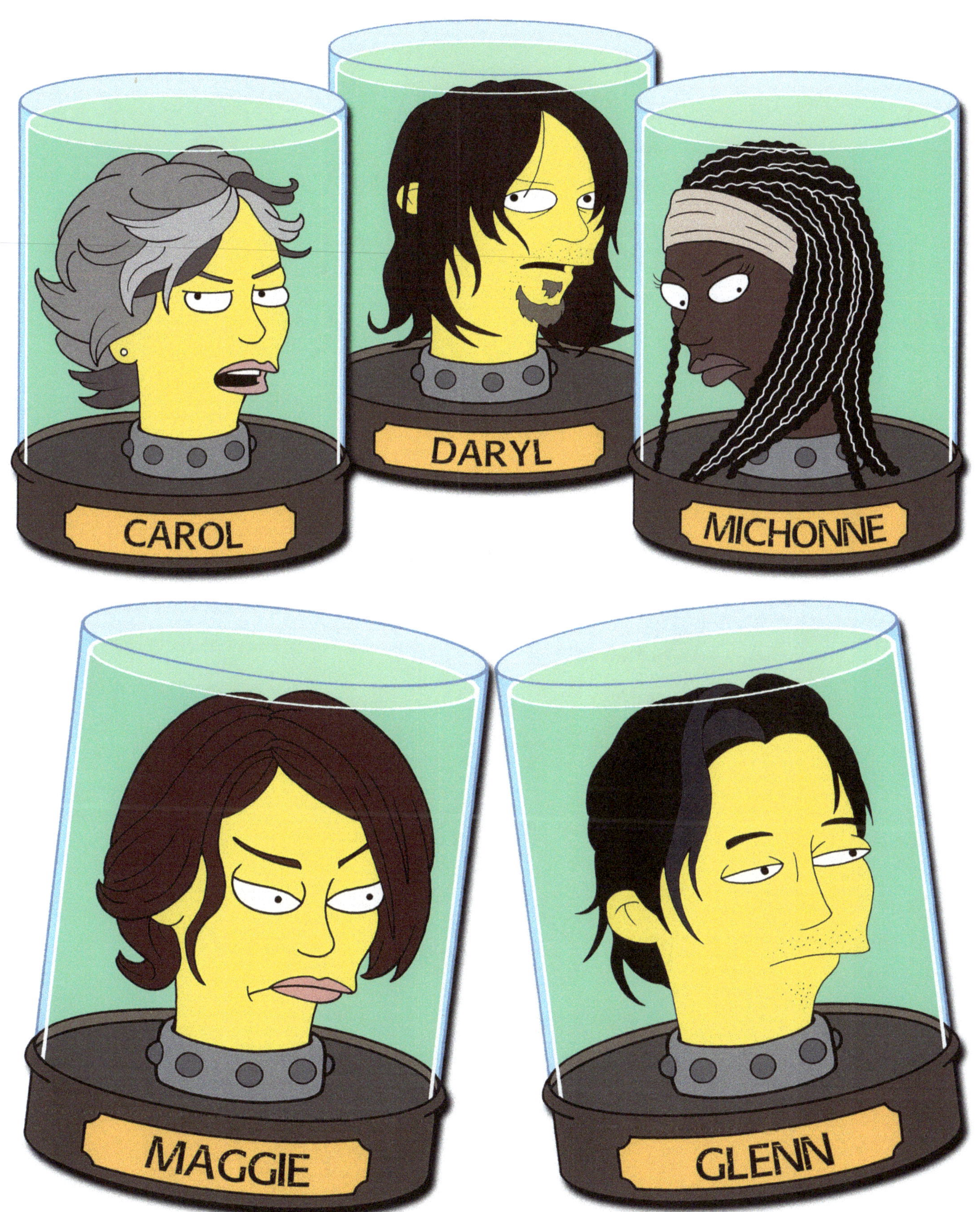

Walking Dead characters from a zombie-plagued Springfield

THANK YOU
FOR YOUR SENSE OF HUMOR
AND SUPPORT.

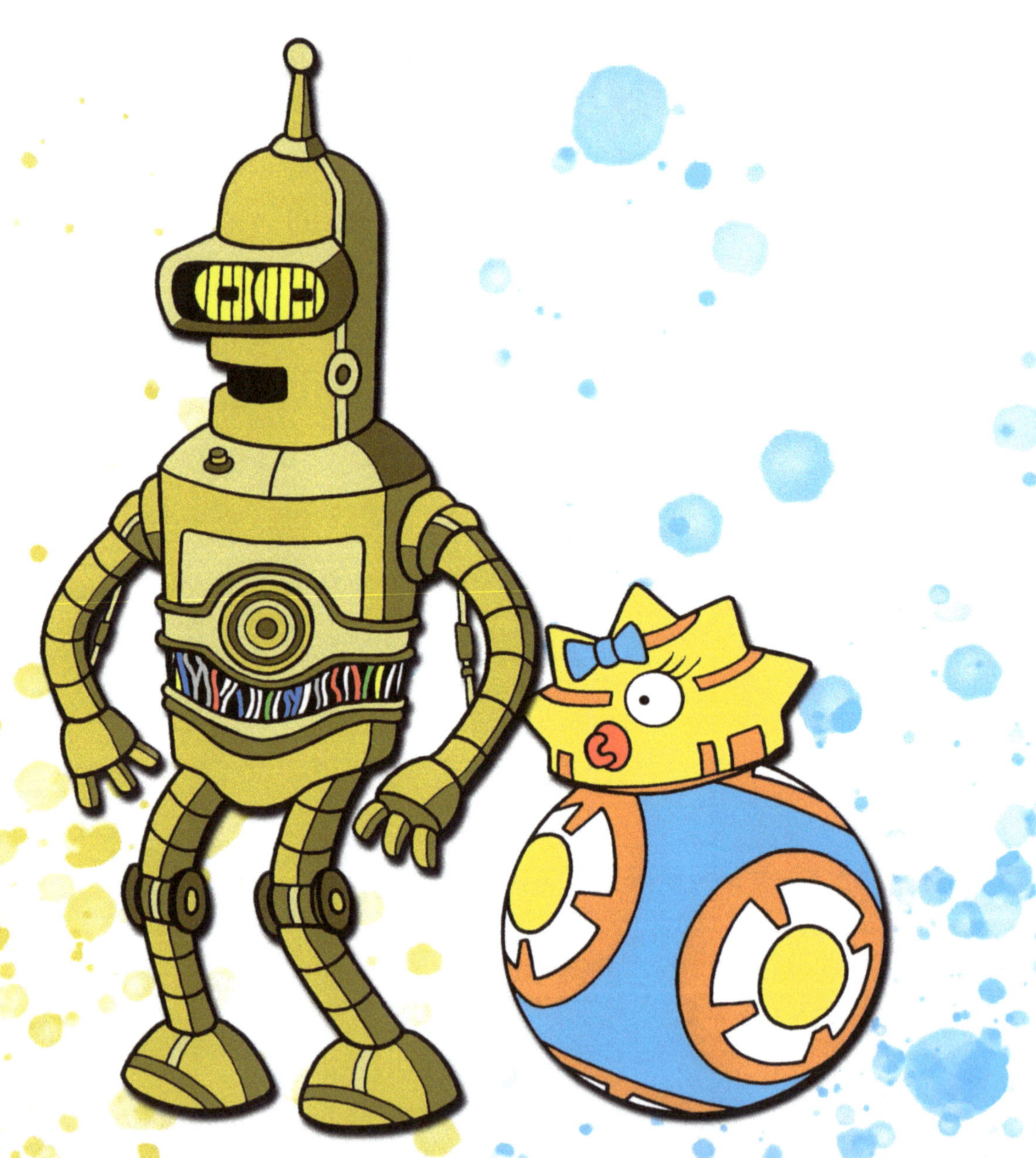

www.ingramcontent.com/pod-product-compliance
Lightning Source LLC
Chambersburg PA
CBHW041038050726
47599CB00018B/2006
* 9 7 8 1 5 1 3 6 4 8 4 9 1 *